The Education of a Novice Ally:

Learning to be a middle-class ally in the work to end poverty

By: Annaka Sikkink

Dedicated to the memory of Gale Allen.
Thank you for your wisdom, love and courage.
Rest in peace.

Contents

Introduction: Seeking Solidarity

Those who authentically commit themselves to the people must re-examine themselves constantly. This conversion is so radical as not to allow of ambiguous behavior... Conversion to the people requires a profound rebirth. Those who undergo it must take on a new form of existence; they can no longer remain as they were.

- Paulo Freire [1]

Like many idealistic college graduates, I left school with high hopes of changing the world, but very little idea where to start. I wanted to create a career and a life that reflected my most deeply held values and contributed to a more just and equal society. I wanted a vocation. And although I had a freshly printed psychology degree, my education up to that point hadn't set me on a clear path to vocation.

Specifically, I wanted a vocation working for economic justice. As I looked around at the social ills of our society—from homelessness to health disparities to educational inequities—it seemed to me that the root cause of many of these things is poverty. Poverty limits access to quality housing in stable neighborhoods. Poverty limits access to adequate medical care. Poverty limits access to school systems that provide excellent education. I figured that once families had access to a livelihood that supported their basic needs and then some, they could afford some choice and influence around most other significant areas of their lives. I still believe this is, if slightly simplistic, basically true.

Surveying the landscape of post-college options, I knew, of course, that there were professions that addressed poverty and economic injustice. I had taken a few social work classes, for instance. I had some friends who were going on to get advanced degrees in public policy or international development. I'd heard of community organizing, and I knew there were people who served the poor from a religious vocation. None of them felt like exactly the right fit for me.

I had also heard of a hidden profession, a tradition that has no name[2], which was in fact the title of a book I had read during my senior seminar. This nameless profession worked within communities to develop the leadership latent there and address social problems in a collaborative way. Its efforts always included and were usually led by individuals experiencing the oppression they were fighting. Though lacking any formal credentials, and thereby often needing to be reinvented from one community to the next, this profession carried on an informal tradition of developmental leadership.[3] It was creative, supportive, and very diverse. Practitioners of the tradition that has no name seemed to have found a way to be allies to one another across the all-too-common divides of class, race, gender or other categories.

That sounded much more like what I felt called to do. I wanted to become a part of that developmental tradition, and pursue my vocation in solidarity with people who had experienced economic injustice. I wanted to come down from the ivory tower to learn how to work in relationship with people who were poor. I wanted to become an ally.

But how do you seek training in a tradition that has no name? You can't get a degree, take a test, or sign up for an apprenticeship in Allyship. So what next?

Over the past decade since graduating from college, I have sought to pursue my vocation in various ways. I traveled for a time, living near and volunteering at the famed Toynbee Hall in East London.[4] After working there, I came back to the states, and volunteered for an advocacy organization called A Minnesota Without Poverty, which aimed to bring about exactly what its name declares. I helped A Minnesota Without Poverty organize public education forums and outreach to young activists on college campuses. A few years later, I got my first paying gig working with families in poverty. I taught high school math in a high-poverty school for a time, and have now spent the last seven years working with families receiving welfare benefits.

All of these experiences have taught me valuable things: about historical trends in poverty alleviation efforts, about the various approaches of government, advocacy organizations, schools and non-profit social services, about the inner functioning (and dysfunctioning) of the poverty industry. And a few things about how to be an ally to people living in poverty in the context of all these kinds of organizations and systems.

However, my overwhelming observation was the <u>lack</u> of authentic solidarity that occurred in most of these contexts. Very few of the places I worked or volunteered had significant degrees of cross-class participation, let alone decision making. Power differentials were endemic—from advocate-citizen, to social service provider-client, to teacher-student, to researcher-subject. That's not to say that there weren't amazing, kind-hearted, dedicated people who wanted to work for justice in the world and who sincerely desired to be allies to one another. But I saw very few organizations that supported those intentions of solidarity or encouraged and developed the leadership of people who had lived in poverty.

Many of the allies I met often seemed to develop allyship partnerships in spite of their professional contexts, rather than because of them.

In response, I wanted to explore the topic of allyship and developmental leadership in a more intentional way. I started doing interviews with a group of activists and service providers from varied class backgrounds about their experiences trying to work in solidarity with others. The interviews quickly evolved into a group that met to explore the topic. We called ourselves the Allyship Project, and met regularly for about a year and a half to discuss the idea of allyship. The Allyship Project was supported by A Minnesota Without Poverty, and the culmination of our conversations was a training that we delivered at a couple of conferences and presented to A Minnesota Without Poverty's board and senior leadership.

The Allyship Project brought together an amazing small group of individuals, who had spent lifetimes advocating for people in poverty both publicly and privately. We had artists, community organizers, social service providers, educators, and community members who built informal webs of support for their neighbors and families. We were a diverse group racially and generationally, although almost all women. And from a class perspective, I was the only member who had lived a consistently middle-class lifestyle and worldview. All the other members of our group had grown up in generational poverty, and most were still struggling economically.

The process of working with the Allyship Project and our honest and deep conversations have by far been the best education on the topic of allyship that a young, middle-class white woman could hope for. The work we did as a group informs every aspect of this book. In fact, I would have been very hesitant to write these words for anything other than my own reflection if it weren't for the wisdom and insight of the community leaders who participated in the Allyship Project with me. Nonetheless, I will say that the interpretation of our discussions reflected in this book are mine and mine alone. It is quite possible that not all the members of the Allyship Project might agree with everything written here.

I also still have an enormous amount to learn, and many lessons I will probably learn the hard way as I try to apply the principles of allyship to my work and vocation. In fact, the most enduring lesson I've learned thus far is how hard solidarity is, and therefore how rarely it authentically occurs. However, there have been other more hopeful lessons, as well, and those are what I am hoping to share here.

What is an ally?

The term "ally" has been used in many different contexts to mean many different things. Of course, the most commonplace usage is geopolitical—allies fight together in times of war, and pursue common interests and common defense when not at war. And although the metaphor is rather violent, the comradery and mutual support of wartime allies is analogous to the experience of authentic allyship in the fight against economic injustice.

Within social justice contexts, the term "ally" is most often used to describe a person who doesn't experience a particular form of oppression but who works with others to combat that oppression (a straight person, for example, working against homophobia).[5] There has been a lot of good work done around the experience of white allies working against racism[6], male allies against sexism[7], and straight allies against homophobia[8]. There are a great many parallels between allyship in these contexts and allyship across economic class. However, there are some unique dynamics of classism and the role of allies, and there aren't as many resources on the topic.[9] Classism is probably one of the least acknowledged "-isms" in American society today, so thinking about how classism operates and how people of economic privilege might be allies against it, lags behind.

Without many external resources from which to build, then, our Allyship Project spent a surprising amount of time wrestling with our definition of an ally. It turned out to be time well spent. The process of refining our definition gave us a solid foundation to understand what we were really talking about as we went on with our work. Our final agreed-upon definition is as follows:

> *An ally is a person who seeks to end poverty, and who partners with people from all class backgrounds to work toward that goal.*

> *An ally develops personal, responsible, respectful and mutually beneficial relationships with people from different class backgrounds than him/herself. These relationships are not necessarily friendships, but are at least respectful working relationships bound together by a common goal of ending poverty.*

One of the first aspects with which we struggled was who should be included in our definition. Unlike most social justice definitions of allyship, we didn't want to restrict ours to only allies of economic privilege. Our group felt that people in poverty, people who had left poverty, people from the middle class, people from the owning class, and so on could all be allies to one another and all had certain things to learn to be effective in those relationships. So we developed a more inclusive definition.

Our second big challenge while crafting our definition was figuring out what differentiated an allyship relationship from any other cross-class relationship. Many members of our group could think of people from different class backgrounds who'd been nice to them or helped them in times of need, sometimes substantially. And while these relationships may have contributed significantly to their lives, we felt that, to be on the level of allyship, people needed to be engaged together in trying to make change in some way. An ally isn't just friendly; an ally has your back in the fight. And an ally isn't just helpful in an altruistic way, but helpful in working toward efforts of mutual interest and benefit.

It must also be acknowledged that some people have grown tired of the term "ally," and feel it has been misapplied to the point of having lost its meaning.[10] I do appreciate these criticisms, and I will address them more comprehensively in the conclusion of this book. I have also tried to incorporate some alternative language throughout my work, such as "acting in solidarity." However, I haven't yet heard a term that can consistently replace "ally" that I prefer. I also think that some of the criticisms come from how allyship is (not) practiced by those who claim the term, and I think the reflections in these pages hopefully address how to practice true allyship.

However, even that statement brings up an important issue. Being a "good" ally is a bit like being a "good" spouse—whether you've succeeded is really up to your partner. You can make every effort, you can read books and attend workshops, but actually being a good spouse is about the quality of the relationship and the subjective experience of both partners. Being an ally works the same way. "Ally" is an honor that must be earned in the context of relationship and bestowed by the people with whom one is in relationship. A person can aspire to be an ally, but they should not declare themselves to be one. This can be especially true for allies from a privileged background who sometimes claim their "allyship" as a defense against their own very un-ally like behavior.[11] Other self-professed allies spend so much time investing in their own personal development that they never get around to actually practicing allyship in relationship with others. This kind of behavior is allyship in name only—not the true practice. We will discuss many more ways to try to actively work in solidary and to aspire to be an ally throughout this book.

When others have honored me with the term ally, I've tried to be very grateful for that gift, but never forgot that I always need to continue to try to earn it.

Seven steps to becoming a better ally

Once we had our definition, the Allyship Project turned to the particulars of becoming an effective ally. We wanted to encourage and facilitate deeper reflection on and practice of allyship. We had many rich discussions and shared many stories of our own cross-class experiences, both the positive and the trying ones. Attempting to distill our conversations, I wrote seven steps to becoming a better ally:

Step 1: Educate yourself on the realities of poverty

Step 2: Educate yourself on oppression and privilege in our society. Examine how you may have internalized oppression and/or privilege that you have experienced

Step 3: Explore how internalized oppression or privilege may affect your behavior in cross-class relationships

Step 4: Seek out opportunities to be in mutually beneficial relationships with people from a different class background than yourself

Step 5: Seek out opportunities to support the leadership of people who have lived or are living in poverty

Step 6: Respect the inherent human dignity and cultural values and practices of everyone

Step 7: Recognize the unique contributions that you can make to the common purpose of ending poverty

The Allyship Project explored these steps in our trainings and workshops, and developed activities to help people engage with the steps and try to figure out how to apply them in their own contexts.

These same seven steps form the structure of the remainder of this book. For each step I will offer explanations on the meaning of the step, reflections on the challenges of practicing it, and experiences that have informed my understanding and attempts to practice them in my own life and career. Hopefully, this will offer some insight to others who seek to enter into the work of bringing about economic justice in an inclusive and responsible way.

I am assuming that you, the reader, already recognize yourself in the first phrase of the definition of an ally: "A person who seeks to end poverty." You may also be much farther along than I am in "partnering with people from all class backgrounds to work toward that goal." But whether mutual, authentic cross-class relationships are something to which you aspire, or something you already have but wish to deepen, I hope to offer something to the conversation. I come to this as a fellow seeker, not an expert practitioner. The Allyship Project itself was a great exercise in building solidarity, but I am still seeking more opportunities in my personal and professional life to build relationships, and I'm sure I have missed opportunities along the way. I am still very much learning even as I share what I've learned thus far in my journey as a novice middle-class ally.

I also hope that whatever class background(s) you identify with, you can find something useful here. Thankfully, the class diversity of our Allyship Project group helped us feel justified in speaking to the experiences of multiple class identities in allyship relationships, so that will hopefully bring balance. (Of course, we certainly didn't reflect all possible experiences and don't want to pretend to speak for everyone.)

That said, I still approach the topic primarily from my own middle-class perspective. I acknowledge that I'm going to have much more to say to my fellow middle-class folks, those of us with economic privilege seeking to be allies in solidarity with others, than to those from other backgrounds. Although our

Allyship Project group felt strongly that everyone has the capacity to be an ally toward everyone else and that all allies have things to learn about how to be fair and kind to one another, the fact remains that there are some unique aspects to being an ally from a privileged background versus being an ally who has experienced oppression. I will elaborate on these aspects throughout this book, and I will try to be explicit when I'm discussing dynamics that primarily affect allies from a particular background.

There's also a second reason to focus on allies from privilege. There's a strong tendency in our society to try to fix poverty by fixing the people in poverty: telling them how they should act, think, speak, dress and so on to be successful. Part of my goal in focusing on instructions for the middle and owning classes is to interrupt this pattern. Privileged people have given people in poverty plenty of instructions already. I don't need to add more. Instead, let's focus on fixing ourselves for a little while.

One note—as the Allyship Project was developing workshops for various trainings and conferences, the Seven Steps became a powerful example of allyship in action. One member of our group, 'Ssence (given name Tottiana Adams), is an amazingly talented spoken word poet and artist. As I read the Seven Steps at one of our planning meetings, she began riffing off of them, interspersing each step with one of her poems. She performed "Can You Hear Me?," a piece about creative integrity and keeping personal control over her art form. That artistic expression of power and dignity meshed amazingly well with the spirit of the steps. We "performed" readings of the Seven Steps and "Can You Hear Me?" a number of times, and the juxtaposition of the wordy, intellectual language of the steps with the powerful emotional tone of the poem made them both more compelling.

Acknowledgments

I have many people who have been important allies and supports to me along the way of exploring, experiencing and writing everything in these pages. Although I can't thank them all, there are many to whom I owe a deep debt of gratitude.

To the members of the Allyship Project: Julia, Marsha, India, Martha, Tottiana ('Ssence), Bambi, and Gale, thank you so much for hanging in there with me. I learned so much from each and every one of you.

To Nancy Maeker and the rest of the Minnesota Without Poverty team, thank you for supporting this vision and for living forward your vision of a state and a world without poverty. If not we, then who, eh?

Thank you to my teachers, especially Joan Ostrove, Phil Sandro, Donna Beegle, Jodi Pfarr, Ben Weiss, Michael Dahl and Zach Charles. Even if you didn't know you were a teacher, you helped me learn something important. You also generously opened yourselves up as fellow seekers, which is the best way of teaching in my opinion.

To my fellow workers in the trenches of the poverty industry: Christine Smith, Kristen Simmons, Katherine Wagoner, and John Klem, thank you for keeping your humanity intact, helping me find mine at times, and for working for others diligently and respectfully.

Finally, thank you to my family for rooting me in my values, and for always believing that I would find a way to make a difference in the world. Thank you, Tim, for your love and support, and for doing the dishes.

With love, gratitude, and hope for a better world,
Annaka

Step 1: Educate Yourself on the Realities of Poverty

An ally should try to learn as much as possible directly from members of communities that have experienced poverty, allowing them to speak in their own words rather than only through economically privileged "experts." At the same time, an ally takes responsibility for her own learning and does not passively wait to be "educated" by people living in poverty.

People living in poverty have been studied a lot. There is an abundant body of literature about the poor, their habits, their geography, their attitudes, and on and on, going back to the Progressive Era.[12] At that time, in the late 1800s, social science was in its infancy, but it has now matured into a well-established academic discipline, complete with competing perspectives and controversies and contested vocabulary[13]. There is a lot of useful research in this literature, much of which has helped galvanize public support for important reforms, and sometimes debunked myths and stereotypes about people living in poverty. (And sometimes helped to create myths and stereotypes, but more on that later.)

What is much harder to find than literature <u>about</u> people living in poverty, is literature <u>by</u> people living in poverty. For allies from economic privilege who don't have first-hand experience with poverty but wish to understand it better, or even for allies who have experienced poverty but wish to know more about the experiences of other races, cultures, or other groups, this can present a challenge. There are, of course, a few made for Hollywood rags-to-riches stories that get a lot of attention. While certainly inspiring, they often reinforce misconceptions about individualism and the American idea of meritocracy[14]. By holding up the plucky few who attain economic mobility, these stories can reinforce stereotypes about the equally plucky, but less lucky, many who don't.

Finding authentic voices from generational poverty can be hard, in print or even in person. It can be especially difficult for allies who were raised in an economically privileged situation. Chances are folks from privilege have been quite insulated from real people who might give them some perspective on poverty. Robert Putman's research has shown that neighborhoods, schools, and even families are increasingly segregated by class[15]. In America in the mid-twentieth century, "affluent kids and poor kids lived near one another, went to school together, played and prayed together, and even dated one another... Nowadays, by contrast, fewer and fewer of us... are exposed in our daily lives to people outside our own socioeconomic niche."[16] In such isolated environments, misunderstandings and mistrust build quickly.

My formative years weren't as segregated as some. I grew up in a town that was small enough and in a house that was close enough to the "bad" part of town that my schools were relatively diverse economically and to a more limited extent, racially. My parents also both came from rural working class backgrounds and were part of the first generation in their families to get college degrees. My mother was actually the only one of her siblings to earn a four-year degree. So I grew up around extended family who had a somewhat different class culture. In fact, when I was very young, my own family experienced a few years of significant economic hardship, when both my parents became unemployed and my mother went through some health challenges. We lost our housing for a short time, and only the generosity of our church community kept us from sliding into a deeper crisis. A member of the church who owned a construction business took my dad onto the crew, and the church helped us pay rent for a little while in our new place.

However, despite that limited exposure to situational poverty, my world growing up was pretty solidly middle-class. Both my parents were college educated. Although my dad worked in the trades as a carpenter, my mom had a professional job as a minister. The families we associated with and the parents of my closest friends were generally highly educated professionals. We lived in a stable, safe, middle-class neighborhood. I never worried as a child about having access to basic needs like food, housing or transportation. I had a lot of exposure to culture and the arts. I was surrounded by encouraging adults who supported my academic work and took my ideas seriously. I had every reason to assume that I would go to college, find some sort of career to support myself, and expect a stable and comfortable lifestyle like the one I grew up in most of the time. Which is, indeed, pretty much how things have turned out so far.

It might, therefore, have been very easy for me to stay isolated from any meaningful relationships with people who had experienced poverty. Luckily, that hasn't been the case, and here I'll share some of the ways in which I developed relationships with people from different class backgrounds, and some of the lessons I learned as a result.

Julia Dinsmore: Meeting a "welfare mother"

My good fortune in escaping class isolation is in large part due to a fateful meeting with an amazing activist, who later became a mentor and dear friend. Julia Dinsmore is an incredible ally to so many who have met her, and I am profoundly grateful to know her. I first met Julia when I was a senior at Macalester College. I was taking a social work course at St. Thomas University, a local affiliated school, and I saw a flyer on their campus for a speech by a "welfare mother." I have no doubt that my life was changed because I happened to see that flyer. Julia's presentation, in a cozy little lounge with a bunch of wide-eyed social work students crammed together on sofas, was electrifying. Here was someone saying out loud so many things that I had long suspected but didn't have the words for. She talked about how well-meaning professionals or providers of charity rarely ever listened to the true needs and wants of those they served. She talked about stigmatization and shaming of people in poverty. She talked about the non-profit industrial complex—how her neighborhood started practicing non-profit prevention, because as more non-profits showed up, the social conditions only got worse! She shared, through her own personal story, how individual and family challenges like mental illness and alcoholism interacted with community issues like access to affordable health care or quality education, which interacted with structural issues like the labor market and child welfare policy, all to create downward spirals of crisis and pain. She spoke in a way both funny and poignant; deeply critical of social injustices but considerate and tender to the naiveté of her young audience who just wanted to help.

After attending that talk at St. Thomas, I invited Julia to Macalester to speak to one of my classes and do a public presentation. Since then, I have had the great privilege to have Julia as a mentor and we have collaborated on many more projects, including the Allyship Project. Indeed, her feedback took the Allyship Project in a whole different direction than I had originally envisioned. I had initially imagined a research project where I would interview different people who had been in ally relationships, but Julia suggested that the topic would be much easier to discuss in a group. She helped recruit the members of our team, always generous with her social connections which span an amazing array of different walks of life. Julia has friends and admirers in every social class, culture, religion and generation, and can't walk into a room without making a few more.

I have learned so much from Julia, and most of the ideas in this book can probably be fully or partially attributed to conversations I've had with her. But I'll begin with the message I took away from that first presentation in a student lounge at St. Thomas. Julia shared her most well-known work, a poem entitled "My Name is Not Those People." She also shared the story of the inspiration for the poem.[*] She wrote it after someone, someone who had every reason and capacity to be an ally to the poor, instead referred to her as "those people" and showed ignorance and insensitivity.[17] Speaking to this potential ally who was too blinded by his own assumptions, Julia asserts, "My name is not 'Those People.' My name is not 'Lazy and Dependent.' My name is not 'Case to be Managed.' My name is not 'Lay Down and Die Quietly.'"

Julia's tenacious defense of her dignity confirmed something very important that I had not heard anyone else explicitly address before. She taught me that there isn't a simple dividing line between the exploiters versus the good guys when it comes to complex economic relationships. Julia wasn't addressing her poem to Mr. Moneybags on a yacht somewhere (although she'd probably have a lot to say to him too). Instead, she was addressing herself to someone who was supposed to be on her side. She was addressing herself to the givers of charity, to the case managers, to the benevolent politicians, who claimed to be looking out for the needs of "those people" but didn't listen to them enough to find out what those needs actually were, or the creative and practical ideas "those people" might have for addressing their needs themselves.

---

[*] It's a great story, but I won't give any more spoilers here. You'll have to read her book if you want to hear it.[17]

Indeed, Julia taught me that sometimes the "good guys" could have even deeper reasons than simple inattention for not listening to "those people." By naming the poverty industry, Julia revealed the unhealthy mix of incentives that can influence an industry which has poverty at the center of its business model. While most people working in the poverty industry are personally benevolent and well intentioned, certain rationalizations and attitudes can start to creep in around the edges of consciousness. "I can try to help the best I can, but I can't change the system." "Poverty will never go away—that's unrealistic." "Those people have too many problems or deficiencies; they're always going to need help." These rationalizations protect the livelihoods of the "good guys" in the poverty industry. So the excuses are all too tempting to believe, even while they discourage the kind of systemic change needed to actually eliminate poverty. After all, it would take some real benevolence to aspire to put oneself out of business!

Hearing Julia so eloquently express her lived experience negotiating the poverty industry, I was able to see more complex nuances to the mainstream approaches to addressing poverty. I could also see, right before me, the sort of talent and articulateness that had been neglected by a system that could really use it. Meeting Julia was a wonderful opportunity to learn about poverty directly from someone who had experienced it. Such lessons are hard to find in the traditional literature about poverty. An ally should always be on the lookout for learning opportunities and encourage and support them.

Learning from clients: Breaking down dichotomies

Julia Dinsmore may have been the first "welfare mother" who I knew as such, but she certainly wasn't the last. In my work over the past seven years, I have had the pleasure to know hundreds of mothers and fathers on welfare. As a job coach and trainer, I helped them prepare for employment, I taught them the language and codes of job seeking, and in some cases, I placed them in temporary internships designed to build skills and connections in the work world. I've found it to be important work that I've enjoyed doing, and I've been able to learn a lot about my clients' lives and the realities of poverty.[†] I very much appreciate how people have let me get a glimpse into their lives, sometimes in small ways, sometimes profound.

Before I move on to some of the lessons I've learned from my clients, I do want to say that as much as I enjoy my work, I would not consider it to be allyship work in and of itself. In my opinion, the welfare system in America is so stingy that it keeps families just on the margins of viability. In fact, even in a relatively generous state like Minnesota, the amount of assistance provided really doesn't meet a family's basic needs without a significant amount of supplemental income or outside support from friends or family, to which most families on welfare do not have [legal] access. As of 2016, the base benefit on MFIP (the Minnesota Family Investment Program) for a parent with one child was $437 per month, which even with food benefits factored in, left families at only 2/3 of the Federal Poverty Guideline. [18] The basic formula for calculating benefits has remained unchanged since 1986, without any adjustment for inflation over those 30 years. [19]

[†] A note on terminology: Many people object to referring to people receiving social services as "clients" because they view it as a dehumanizing, pejorative term. Indeed, in my day to day work I usually refer to people in my training classes as "participants" or "students." However, here, I feel it is beneficial to be honest about the fact that we are all dealing with a dehumanizing system which does refer to people as "clients." So I use the term not to insult the individuals with whom I work, but to highlight how rarely we listen to our "clients." We rarely allow them to teach us about the systems in which we co-exist, or even about their own lives and experiences.

With this limited assistance, the welfare system helps a few industrious souls find the resources to move into stable careers, but for most it provides inadequate help that comes with a ton of strings attached. Therefore, on the whole it is a poverty mitigation system, not a poverty eradication system. In this context, I don't feel that my work was allyship work, even though I always tried to approach my relationships with individuals with the care and ethic of an ally.

One of the most enduring lessons from working with families in the welfare system has been the complexity of the causes of poverty. American ideologies define the causes of poverty primarily (sometimes exclusively) in one of two ways. One camp believes that poverty is a result of individual deficiencies or misfortunes—poor moral choices, mental illness, chemical dependency, lack of work ethic, etc. This view is very compatible with our cultural belief in the importance of hard work and individualism, and, most significantly, in the opportunity available to everyone if they "work hard and play by the rules." This view is also very compatible with the way our work-fare system is designed. Most of the emphasis is placed on helping individuals cope with whatever difficult circumstances may have come their way, or resolving any skill deficiencies or "dysfunctional" attitudes that prevent them from getting or maintaining employment.

The competing view is that poverty is a deficiency of our economic system, and that faulty governmental policy, global economic forces, or, according to some, even the structure of capitalism itself, condemns some portion of the population to life on the margins. From this perspective, the solutions to poverty lie in economic development, large scale redistribution and education and training, rather than individual behavior change. It's not hard to see how these differing perspectives line up with the basic ideologies of the left and right ends of the political spectrum.

It should be said that some people focus on a third, usually less polarizing view of poverty, situating it in local communities, where factors such as neighborhood economic development, the quality of the educational system, crime and policing patterns, access to resources like health care, and community cohesion work together to create or negate poverty.[20] Often this kind of community perspective is tinged with either an individualistic or systemic lens as well, but it can also be its own post on the continuum.

For myself, I came into my work with families in poverty well convinced that poverty is a systemic issue. I had grown up in a pretty liberal family where conversations about systemic injustices weren't unusual. Then I attended a predominantly left-leaning college with a strong tradition of political activism and analysis. In college I had read and sympathized with lots of sociology texts with a Marxist bent, and I had written papers denouncing the "blame the victim" approach of demonizing single mothers on welfare. So I had pitched my tent squarely in the systemic camp.

Having now gotten to know a lot more single mothers than I had when I wrote papers about them, I still think that demonizing them and their families is a grossly cheap tactic. But I've also seen the real pain and human cost of some of the "moral" issues and "family values" associated with poverty. I'll never forget, during a parenting discussion group, listening to a group of single moms reflect on the challenges of navigating the difficult questions their children ask about their absent dads. That, in turn, led to a conversation about the pain of not having known their own fathers. On other occasions, I talked with many young adults who regretted earlier choices to drop out of school or get pregnant young, and now had to deal with the challenge of raising a family while developing a career. I met young fathers struggling to figure out how to parent since their parents had been absorbed in drugs or alcohol or other forms of self-destruction. I saw the difficulty individuals had finding employment or housing after an impulsive choice to escalate an altercation or to shoplift burdened them with a criminal record.

I definitely don't believe that these types of behaviors and choices are the sole or even primary causes of poverty, and by no means are they exclusive to people living in poverty. Plenty of middle-class and owning-class young adults make regrettable choices, and issues like domestic violence or substance abuse occur in all walks of life. But when people in poverty find themselves in these situations, they have far fewer resources to deal with the consequences. I've heard too many stories where a decent lawyer might have helped someone avoid a life-altering guilty plea. Poor young adults who drop out of college accrue a student loan burden that they may never dig out of, which in a middle-class family might have been a bill for Mom and Dad. And parenting, though a tough job for anyone, is easier with a supportive and safe community and access to resources to benefit one's family.

There are also some of these problems that do seem to occur with greater frequency in poor communities. Family structure is a real concern, not just a spiteful stereotype or scapegoat. Raising a family with one income and at the same time providing all the other non-financial support a family needs is an arduous task. Census data shows that almost half of children in a household headed by a single mother live in poverty, an astoundingly high proportion.[21] Incidentally, out of wedlock pregnancy is a perfect example of an issue where actually talking to people reveals a deeper interpretation than common middle-class assumptions. Most middle or owning-class observers would be likely to assume that an unplanned pregnancy is a turning point, a diversion <u>away</u> from priorities and productive goals. However, many young women with whom I worked credited their pregnancy and birth of their child as indeed a turning point, but one that helped them set priorities and approach life in a more mature way. This is also supported by the excellent book *Promises I Can Keep*[22], which is based on interviews with single mothers on welfare. The authors found that an unplanned pregnancy is usually a symptom of a life that was already headed in a dangerous direction, or not much of a direction at all. Single parenthood, rather than being a direct cause of poverty, is a result of it, and often sparks the motivation for personal growth, even if the circumstances are now more complicated for young parents to pursue education and careers with babies in tow.

In sum, my clients have taught me a more balanced perspective on the causes of poverty. It's not an either-or proposition—individual versus structural causes. Global forces impact individual choices; community structure impacts political outcomes; families contribute to strong communities, or the reverse. So for an ally, the appropriate approach is to seek to understand all levels of influence, from the macro to the micro. I now consider more deeply the individual actions or circumstances of the families who I work with, not to judge or shame their characters, but with compassion for the undeniable hurt they have experienced. And when those harmful personal choices may have been avoidable, I try to avoid assumptions about the causes or meanings of those choices. But I no longer deny their existence, or think of them as overblown propaganda from insensitive pundits. To do so would be to discount the genuine reality of families in poverty, with its messy mix of the personal, the political, the admirable, the regrettable, the hopeful and the painful.

Stigmatization: The dangers of well-intentioned research

Hopefully my examples demonstrate the importance of seeking to learn about poverty from a variety of sources, prioritizing direct interaction and relationship with people who have experienced poverty. That's not to negate many other valuable resources about poverty from academic social science and elsewhere. By all means, the mainstream research is a great place to start. It can often provide unique forms of analysis that connect poverty to other disciplines and issues like politics, economic trends, social movements, psychology, or educational theory.[23] And the hard facts and statistics are often necessary to have when seeking support and funding for resources to alleviate poverty.

That said, respected theories have sometimes been turned on themselves and against people living in poverty. For instance, research done in mid-century on the "culture of poverty" was originally intended to show the destructive effects of systemic economic problems.[24] A number of sociologists argued that adverse economic conditions and societal discrimination could become entrenched in cultural patterns and value systems, and thus become self-perpetuating. Although these theories, culminating in the well-known Moynihan Report in 1965, had their critics at the time, they were also highly influential in mobilizing the ambitious War on Poverty.[25]

Later on, however, the idea of a culture of poverty fed into the stereotypes of the less sympathetic. Many of those opposed to governmental assistance used the culture of poverty theory to argue that people in poverty were substantively different from other Americans, had inferior value systems, and were thus beyond help.[26] Ultimately, the culture of poverty theory inadvertently helped create the destructive cultural icon of the welfare queen, and a policy backlash against families in poverty. "Poverty experts have proved to be rather ineffective cultural brokers: even when offered in the name of social criticism or as a call to action, their formulations of cultural deviance have been used far more readily and regularly to stigmatize, isolate, and deny assistance to the poor."[27]

One branch of current scholarship may have the potential to go the way of the Moynihan Report, I fear. Much attention has been paid in recent years to early traumatic experiences and their effect on the development of the brain and cognition.[28] Although not necessarily class specific, some of this research has shown that children in poverty are more likely to experience more forms of trauma, and therefore suffer the adverse health consequences and cognitive deficiencies associated. Recent research in neuroscience, in fact, claims to show visible underdevelopment of the brain associated with poverty.[29] So far, this sort of research is generally being used to argue for systemic policies to combat poverty and to provide supportive education that can help children raised in poverty catch up. But I fear it could easily become warped to support vicious stereotypes about people in poverty being less intelligent, less able to learn, or generally less capable than others. While modern neuroscience has shown amazing capacity of our brains to adapt and replenish themselves,[30] it is still a pretty damning statement to tell someone that the very structure of their brain is lacking.

While no researcher should be expected to have perfect foresight into how his or her work might be misinterpreted by those hostile to its aims, these examples do point out how important it is to be wary of the stigmatization that can so easily occur. Any attempt to explain characteristics or tendencies of people in poverty can all too easily get twisted into generalizations and stereotypes. The casual reader of research or theories about poverty (including this work that you're reading right now) should also remain thoughtful about the possible biases or assumptions that may be reflected in the work, or which could be imposed upon it from the outside.

How to educate oneself on poverty

By getting to know people in poverty and hearing accounts and analysis directly from them, allies can balance the sometimes harsh and impersonal science with the human immediacy of real stories—sometimes painful, sometimes inspiring, sometimes enraging. But all with their own truth to share. Hearing such stories can help allies hopefully avoid the tendency to over-generalize or to harden theories into prejudices. It does take some work to seek out narratives, to develop relationships, to keep your eyes open for flyers about the person who may become your next mentor. I've suggested some further reading, including resources from Julia Dinsmore and other individuals who have lived in poverty.[31] But no book can replace the depth of relationship, so finding in-person mentors is important.

It is also important as an ally to educate oneself in a respectful way. Not everyone who lives or lived in poverty may wish to share their story with others, at least not until some mutual trust has been built and <u>both</u> parties have had a chance to share their stories. When talking to someone face-to-face, the best strategy is to ask respectfully, but allow someone a gracious way to say no, and to be sensitive to body language that may show that someone is uncomfortable. Our society heaps a lot of shame on people who have survived poverty, so many people may be "in the closet" about their class experiences. Many people from privilege may also be uncomfortable sharing their realities as well, not wanting to brag or seem insensitive. We'll talk more in future chapters about how people from all class backgrounds can help counter the shame and discomfort and how we can all move beyond awkwardness to appreciating and sharing the strengths and benefits of our origins.

One particular note about sensitivity: many times in social service settings, it is institutional policy to ask someone who is basically a perfect stranger deeply personal questions about their past, their intimate relationships, their fears and challenges and so on. As a result, I've noticed that many of my clients have become pretty numb to this invasion of their privacy and dignity, and may be extremely open to sharing. However, I've always tried to remain sensitive to avoid asking anyone questions which, if our roles were reversed, I might be uncomfortable answering. This is especially important since I know that professional "boundaries" protect me from ever having to answer those questions myself.

Lastly, it is important for allies to take responsibility for our own education, and not be passive about it. Betsy Leondar-Wright talks about "wannabe wimp" allies in the context of combatting sexism.[32] A wannabe wimp ally will talk all day long about his abstract support for feminism, but hasn't educated himself well enough about women's lived experience to be helpful in the immediate term. He does not even attempt to look at the world from the perspective of a woman, or ask her for her perspective. So he will attend a meeting about equity, but never offer a woman a ride home, not bothering to consider that she might have to walk home alone on dark streets. Instead he will passively wait to be asked.

Similarly, I've heard people of color express frustration with white "allies" who don't take any personal responsibility for learning about racism.[33] Sometimes we allies want to put the entire onus on people of color to educate us. "How can we learn if you won't teach us?," we say. But the reality is there are a thousand ways to learn, from reading books to watching movies to just observing carefully. Expecting our allies to be solely responsible for educating us puts a heavy practical and emotional burden on them. They can never know exactly how a privileged person will react if they try to challenge oppressive attitudes and misinformation. Educating others can be risky business, so we shouldn't assume that our allies will be willing to do it, or even that it should be their responsibility.

Ideally, those of us who have had the privilege to ignore oppression should have the responsibility to learn about it. We will still have wannabe wimp moments, when we are confronted with a situation that teaches us something we had never considered before and never would have thought to ask. But an ally who takes responsibility for his own education will be on the lookout for opportunities to consider the perspective of allies from other backgrounds, to find ways to learn what he doesn't know, and respectfully and openly ask more about it when necessary.

Step 2: Educate Yourself on Oppression and Privilege in our Society

Everyone in our society has been exposed to stereotypes and misinformation about ourselves and others. An ally should always be on the lookout for ways in which he may have come to believe these lies, consciously or unconsciously, and challenge that internalization in himself.

Let's say I were to describe someone as "privileged." What mental image would come to mind? Luxury and leisure? Arrogance and greed? Sophistication and culture? Take a moment to think about it. Who do you see when you picture a "privileged" person?

Whatever your mental image, it probably doesn't represent your daily lived experience. However, most of us actually do experience some form of privilege every day, even if we wouldn't call ourselves "privileged." For our purposes here, privilege refers to unearned advantages or benefits that someone receives as a result of some aspect of their identity, such as race, class, gender, sexual orientation, physical ability, religion, etc. [34]   Privilege is conferred by society whether we ask for it or not. And it isn't necessarily a gross excess of advantage; privilege may simply be the way we'd like for all people to be treated.

For example, as a white person, if I get hired for a job, others will likely assume that I was hired because of my merit, not because of some diversity goal or quota that my company was trying to fulfill. Even though this may simply seem fair, it is actually a privilege conferred by my race. A person of color may not be afforded the same confidence from her new colleagues, in which case she would be experiencing oppression—the opposite of privilege. Recognizing the unfairness of her experience requires me to acknowledge the privilege of my own experience.

At the same time, privilege is not all or nothing. Most of us have aspects of our identities that are discriminated against by the broader culture, so we simultaneously experience a confusing mix of oppression and advantage. A person may be male, and also Latino. A person may be white, and also gay. A person may be wealthy, and also have a disability. Context can matter a great deal, as well, to which aspect of our identity gets the most attention. For instance, with my previous example, if my new job was in a male dominated profession like construction, my racial privilege might be overshadowed by my gender oppression, and I may no longer get the default respect of my coworkers.

So privilege and oppression can be contradictory and contextual, and therefore sometimes hard to recognize in our complex society. Privilege, especially, can be hard to acknowledge in oneself. It just sounds so, well, privileged! We don't want to be spoiled or haughty. We didn't ask for our privilege, and we don't want to be judged by it. To make matters worse, one of the privileges of privilege can be the ability to ignore or deny the existence of privilege. But it is still there, as much as we try not to see it.

Moreover, <u>class</u> oppression and privilege may be even more difficult to identify than that based on race or gender or other identity categories, for a couple of reasons. Many people still believe America to be a class-less society, or even if they acknowledge class, they don't locate themselves anywhere other than the ubiquitous middle. Research has shown that over 80% of Americans identify themselves as middle class.[35] So if nearly everyone considers themselves part of the "normal" middle, it can be hard to detect privilege or oppression operating. Further, even if individuals have a developed class identity, it is, in many cases, an invisible identity and a malleable one. It's not always easy to tell to what class someone belongs or may have belonged in the past. By extension, it quickly becomes thorny trying to figure out if a particular experience or interaction is based in class oppression or privilege, or some other cultural identity, or just personality.

Recognizing, then, the particularities and complexities of individual experience, we can still zoom out to see the workings of class oppression and privilege at a broader level. Many aspects are systemic and institutional. For instance, as any family who's ever looked for housing knows, one of the biggest determinants in housing pricing is the quality of the school district.[36] When families in poverty are not able to afford high-quality housing (or in many cases, any stable housing at all), they are simultaneously missing out on educational opportunities, a sense of safety and security in their neighborhood, and possibly even a fundamental level of trust in other human beings.[37] The inability to afford one particular resource sets in motion a complex interplay of disadvantages. Conversely, when economically privileged families can afford housing in "good" neighborhoods, they can set future generations up for many advantages far beyond the roof over their heads. Zoning laws, financing practices, school funding policies and inherited wealth have created and reinforce class segregated residential patterns across the country, and these system level patterns have huge implications for the lives of individuals.[38]

Then there are personal and internal dimensions to privilege and oppression. When I think back on my own childhood, I can think of a number of examples of privilege. Because I was raised by white, middle-class, college-educated parents, there were certain advantages that I received and continue to receive. For instance, I started school with a very well developed vocabulary for a five year old. Some possible implications of that: my teachers probably thought of me as very intelligent and gave me additional positive encouragement or challenge. Throughout my education, I was recognized and rewarded for my academic work. I was given leadership positions like being president of our honor society in high school. I was allowed to break the rules. For example, I was able to go off campus during lunches and study halls because I was a trusted "good kid." I was accepted into a top tier private college, and went for four years even though it was ridiculously expensive. I didn't have the privilege of having college paid for, but based on my parents' experience and encouragement, I went on faith that I would later earn income adequate to pay down my student loans. (For that matter, my parents had good credit and assets to co-sign my student loans. And their financial security was due, to a degree, to their class and race privilege.) After college, I was able to travel internationally and support myself by getting a well-paying tutoring job based on my SAT scores. How had I scored so well on the SATs? In part by having really good grammar and vocabulary that was taught to me by my parents and was my natural way of speaking since I was five years old. [39]

Obviously, all of these life events also required significant hard work and dedication on my part, and support and encouragement on my family's part. So it isn't as though class and race simply handed me my successes. There was a lot of hard work. But it would have been a lot harder if I had been trying to catch up to my peers in kindergarten rather than starting out ahead. And it would have been a lot harder if my teachers had assumed I was less capable because my parents lived on the "wrong side of town," or because my skin was a different color, or because my primary language was not English. My teachers and other adults in my life believed in me, and throughout my growing up years I absorbed those positive messages and I believed in myself too.

In that way, I internalized some of my privilege. I also internalized biases and stereotypes about others different from me, including my classmates who lived in the gang afflicted "bad part of town." They doubtless had stereotypes about me, too, and had probably also internalized some of the stereotypes about themselves. We are all exposed to these messages from our formative years, and part of our task as allies is to recognize and challenge the internalizations within ourselves.

Three theorists in particular have been helpful to me as I've undertaken the internal work of scrutinizing my own biases and assumptions. Paulo Freire, Donna Beegle, and Maria Yellow Horse Brave Heart came from very different places and times, but all are part of the hidden tradition of developmental leadership and education, and all share a passionate commitment to overcoming poverty and oppression.

Paulo Freire: Oppressor guilt

Paulo Freire's landmark book, *Pedagogy of the Oppressed*, is an unmatched classic in the area of oppression and class theory. Freire was an educator in Brazil, and developed much of his philosophy of oppression while teaching illiterate peasants how to read, hence the pedagogy in his title. He taught much more than simple A-B-C's however. He used literacy instruction as a vehicle to teach a critical consciousness, or *conscientização,*[40] to help the oppressed understand their world in a deeper way and begin to see the systemic causes of their hardships, hence the second half of his title. Freire believed in humanism to the deepest degree: he believed in trusting the intelligence and ingenuity of the oppressed above all else. Furthermore, he believed that society would ultimately be transformed by revolution, and that only the oppressed could be the legitimate instigators and heirs of that revolution. We will explore many more of Freire's ideas throughout this book.

Paulo Freire presents class oppression in a predominantly binary way—either one is oppressed or an oppressor. In his rural Latin American context, where society was largely made up of landowners and peasants, that probably made a lot of sense. However, in modern American society, where class is diffuse and multi-layered and contestable, it's harder to see things quite so starkly. To complicate things further, within our multiple identities, most people are simultaneously oppressed and oppressor.

Nonetheless, even if we acknowledge our layered identities, there's still something important to confront in Freire's language. For those of us who have been granted privilege in one or more of our identities (particularly for the purposes of this conversation—class privilege), we've already discussed how it can be uncomfortable enough to acknowledge one's own privilege. But then to be told that privilege is not even the worst of it—we are in fact <u>oppressors</u>. Freire doesn't mince words when he talks about oppressors, either. "The oppressors, who oppress, exploit, and rape by virtue of their power, cannot find in this power the strength to liberate either the oppressed or themselves."[41] Ouch. Who would want to recognize herself in that?

According to Freire, there aren't even benevolent oppressors:

> Any attempt to "soften" the power of the oppressor in deference to the weakness of the oppressed almost always manifests itself in the form of false generosity; indeed the attempt never goes beyond this. In order to

have the continued opportunity to express their "generosity," the oppressors must perpetuate injustice as well. An unjust social order is the permanent fount of this "generosity," which is nourished by death, despair and poverty. [42]

Slightly more mercifully, Freire does offer one way out of the oppressor role, but he goes to great lengths to stress the difficulty and rarity of it:

Certain members of the oppressor class join the oppressed in their struggle for liberation... Theirs is a fundamental role, and has been so throughout the history of the struggle. It happens, however, that as they cease to be exploiters or indifferent spectators, or simply the heirs of exploitation and move to the side of the exploited, they almost always bring with them the marks of their origin: their prejudices and their deformations, which include a lack of confidence in the people's ability to think, to want, and to know. Accordingly, these adherents to the people's cause constantly run the risk of falling into a type of generosity as malefic as that of the oppressors... Our converts truly desire to transform the unjust order; but because of their background they believe that they must be the executors of the transformation. They talk about the people, but they do not trust them... A real humanist can be identified more by his trust in the people which engages him in their struggle, than by a thousand actions in their favor without that trust. [43]

Freire goes on to say that such an ally must "re-examine themselves constantly" and undergo "a profound rebirth." For Freire, working with and on behalf of the oppressed is not for the faint of heart.

So how do we respond to all of this exacting rhetoric? Does having economic privilege really make me an oppressor who "oppresses, exploits, and rapes" my way through the world?

And if I wish to renounce that, do I truly have to be reborn and convert to a new level of consciousness?

On the one hand, no. Such dramatic language overstates the situation and could lead an ally into soul-smothering guilt and despair. On the other hand, there is indeed a lot of work and struggle involved in understanding the "marks of one's origin." Striving for true solidarity requires more of a commitment than most think. We will continue to explore ways to seek to do that throughout this book. For instance, Freire has much more to say to allies than just to berate them about being oppressors, so we will return to his (and others') theories and instructions many times in the chapters ahead.

But first, let's address the topic of guilt and shame,‡ which will inevitably come up as we try to wrap our minds around being oppressors. Feeling ashamed is likely to happen, but not likely to be helpful.[44] Members of the Allyship Project all agreed, unequivocally, that guilt is not a useful emotion in the context of allyship. All people are, to use Freire's words, "heirs of exploitation" no matter what our class background. Having privilege, or suffering oppression, is a product of a social structure much larger and longer established than ourselves. Our particular circumstances should not be a source of shame any more than any other accident of birth.

Anne Bishop writes that our over-individualized culture makes it more likely that we will struggle with guilt while learning about oppression.[45] We tend to believe that our

------

‡ Brené Brown has done a lot of interesting work on guilt and shame, although from an individual, psychological standpoint, not from the perspective of social oppression. She differentiates between guilt—a useful, temporary emotion that is a response of our conscience to morally wrong action—and shame—a pervasive feeling of inadequacy that impacts our sense of self and is usually out of proportion to the source. I appreciate her characterization, so although I'm using the two terms somewhat interchangeably here, I'm referring more to shame as she defines it. [44]

individual actions, or even just the intent of our actions, is all that matters. So, we get stuck thinking either that we couldn't possibly be oppressors, because we don't intend to be, or, instead, that the continued existence of oppression must be evidence of our personal failure. Denial or guilt become our only unhealthy options.

Conversely, a more collective and structural understanding of society allows us to acknowledge the inevitability of our own privilege without being crushed by guilt.

> All members of this society grow up surrounded by oppressive attitudes; we are marinated in it. It runs in our veins; it is as invisible to us as the air we breathe. I do not believe anyone raised in Western society can ever claim to have finished ridding themselves completely of their oppressive attitudes. It is an ongoing task... So, until we succeed in making a more humane world, yes, we are racist (or ageist, or classist, or heterosexist, and so forth). Understanding this is part of learning to think structurally rather than individually.[46]

We have a personal and collective responsibility to try to combat oppression, but as individuals the best we will probably ever accomplish is to be oppressors "in recovery." We don't need to feel ashamed of that.

Shame not only causes unjustified personal pain and discomfort, but it can impair and distort the practice of allyship too. Allies hampered by undue shame of their privilege are more likely to exhibit Freire's false generosity. "Discovering himself to be an oppressor may cause considerable anguish, but it does not necessarily lead to solidarity with the oppressed. Rationalizing his guilt through paternalistic treatment of the oppressed, all the while holding them fast in a position of dependence, will not do."[47] When people are primarily motivated by reducing their own guilt, or seeking gratitude in order to make themselves feel better, then the aim is no longer justice, it is self-assuagement.

Sometimes this can lead allies to provoke victim behavior or to expect excessive gratitude. This is false generosity because it strengthens the power differential between people of different backgrounds. The privileged ally always gets to hold the threat of walking away if the oppressed ally isn't grateful enough, or doesn't seem needy enough, or asserts their own authority.

Alternatively, privileged allies motivated by shame may become doormats, gullible and passive around people who have experienced oppression. This isn't very useful to anyone, either. A doormat ally can easily get taken advantage of, unintentionally or otherwise, by individuals in poverty. And a doormat is not authentically bringing their own strengths and judiciousness to the challenges of ending poverty, so their allies from poverty are not getting the advantage of true partners and contributors to the struggle.[48] Part of the work of all allies is encouraging the leadership of people in poverty (see Step Five) but that does not mean that everyone else should roll over and play dead.

Doormat allies can also be rather disingenuous. In "A Critique of Ally Politics," the author M. maintains that "allies" from privilege often passively follow the suggestions of anyone from an oppressed group. By doing so they are not authentically sharing leadership; they are in fact avoiding accountability:

> To be an ally is to shirk responsibility for your own actions—legitimizing your position by taking the voice of someone else, always acting in someone else's name. It's a way of taking power while simultaneously diminishing your own accountability, because not only are you hiding behind others but you're also obscuring the fact that you're in control of making the choices about who you're listening to.[49]

I would disagree that <u>all</u> allies will inevitably do this, but I do recognize that it is a distinct danger when we are operating primarily out of shame. We are fooling ourselves if we let our guilty conscience convince us that we can't have any opinions. We do have opinions, starting with, as M. points out, opinions about with whom we want to ally ourselves and from whom we want to learn. Those choices will fundamentally shape our work, and it is important that we take responsibility and ownership of those decisions, with humility but without shame.

So in one way or another, shame distorts people's humanity and relationships wherever it pops up. It is not a useful emotional response to poverty and oppression. That said, poverty is a deeply lamentable human invention, and it causes unrelenting pain and hardship. Some sort of emotion is inevitable when we honestly confront poverty's destruction. So, then, what kind of emotional response is more useful than shame?

I can think of three suggestions. First, anger. In my middle-class, northern European culture, anger is not something easily acknowledged, not in public anyway. But when anger motivates to action, when it is indignation that leads to an unwillingness to accept injustice any longer, then it is an extraordinarily useful and admirable emotion. I believe Paulo Freire's ferocious rhetoric, even though it initially seems so damning to the oppressor class, actually comes from this kind of constructive anger. In fact, he describes how the emergence of consciousness among the oppressed and their subsequent rebellion will be an act of <u>love</u> toward all humanity, oppressors included. "As the oppressors dehumanize others and violate their rights, they themselves also become dehumanized. As the oppressed, fighting to be human, take away the oppressors' power to dominate and suppress, they restore to the oppressors the humanity they had lost in the exercise of oppression."[50] Eventually, Freire hopes for society to progress toward an era not of vengeance toward oppressors, but of love and humanity restored.

A second appropriate response to poverty is sorrow. As allies get to know one another and hear each other's stories of dehumanization, sad and difficult realities will inevitably surface. Allies should guard against pity, which objectifies people into their suffering. But compassion and empathy with fellow humans experiencing suffering is a natural and appropriate human response.

Finally, allies can channel their frustration with poverty away from paralyzing shame and into honest and humble self-examination. Although none of us should feel personally liable for the state of our society, we are personally responsible for trying to influence that society, starting with seeking an understanding of our own position within it and how that has affected our worldview.[51] Allies must seek self-awareness and humility to recognize that none of us can effect a just social order alone. It can only be accomplished by working together in solidarity. Privileged allies cannot impose "solutions" on people in poverty and expect them to work. Leaving someone out of their own liberation is a contradiction—liberation has already been negated by not respecting the right to self-determination and dignity.[52] Nor can allies in poverty succeed alone, for many of the same reasons.

Even though Freire insisted that revolutionary change must start with the oppressed, he also acknowledged the crucial role of allies, his "true converts." Privileged allies may be able to understand and influence society's power structures by virtue of having had greater access to them, and in some cases they may have an easier task reaching consciousness of oppression by not having suffered under it to the same extent. We need each other in the process of re-humanizing ourselves and developing an economic system that preserves the humanity of all.

Donna Beegle: The lessons that poverty teaches

If "oppressors" have an arduous task coming to self-awareness without sinking into shame, people who have experienced class oppression may have an even greater challenge. For centuries, Western societies have blamed the poor for their poverty, or at least the segment of the poor deemed "undeserving."[53] American society follows right along in this tradition. As we discussed in Step One, Americans tend to hold a predominantly individualistic view of the causes of poverty, attributing it to personal moral choices and characteristics, like laziness or addiction. If we primarily believe in these causes of poverty, then the responsibility and the culpability lies fully with the individual living in poverty. In fact, America's unmatched intensity of blaming and shaming of people in poverty can be baffling to observers from other countries.[54]

One of my favorite crusaders against poverty shame is Dr. Donna Beegle. Beegle is a trainer, researcher, and writer who grew up in generational poverty herself, and has now devoted her career to helping individuals and institutions understand poverty better and be effective in combatting it. I had the wonderful opportunity to attend a four-day training with her in her hometown of Portland, Oregon, and came away with some valuable concepts and language.

Donna Beegle frames her understanding of poverty's impact on individuals as "lessons that poverty teaches." I greatly appreciate this language, for a few reasons. I love how non-judgmental it is, in contrast to shaming language about "character deficiencies" or a "dysfunctional culture" of poverty. By contrast, someone who has learned lessons from life is generally regarded as wise, or at least thoughtfully responsive to their environment and experience. Beegle concurs that the lessons that poverty teaches are generally reasonable and self-preserving in the context of poverty, although she acknowledges that some are very painful and may become counter-productive in other contexts.[55]

When that is the case, the second essential quality of lessons learned comes into play—lessons learned can be unlearned or replaced with new ones. Unlearning lessons isn't always easy, because they may be deeply ingrained and beyond conscious awareness, but it is possible. This is why I greatly prefer Beegle's model to that of a culture of poverty. Rather than condemning people in poverty as permanently pathological, this model recognizes them as adaptive to certain conditions, but also shows how people can adapt further when conditions change.

Before we examine a few examples of lessons that poverty teaches, it is important to note that not everyone will internalize these lessons in the same way. Some individuals will respond differently to their environments, and their environments may also vary. For instance, author and activist bell hooks talks about growing up in a small racially segregated community. There, hooks felt a sense of racial solidarity that softened class distinctions. She was also taught a strict religious ethic of care for the poor and recognition that "the poor were God's chosen people—that poverty should not be a cause of shame."[56] In that community, then, people in poverty might not have learned the same lessons as those in a more antagonistic urban setting. Therefore, as is true any time that we talk about common themes of human experience, it is important not to generalize too broadly.

Nevertheless, there are common lessons that are usually learned in a context of poverty. In Donna Beegle's training we learned that low wage work is usually unreliable, demeaning, and inadequate to meet the needs of oneself or one's family.[57] Consequently, poverty teaches that the only reliable outcome of having a job is that it will take time away from one's family. A job doesn't mean stability, nor achievement, just stress and isolation. For someone who grew up, like Beegle did, in a family and community with low levels of education and poor wages, this makes perfect sense. Her parents usually worked (when they could find work) as migrant farm laborers, and it never earned enough to meet basic needs. So coming from this family context, when a young Donna Beegle heard her teachers tell her to graduate from high school so she could get a job someday, the incentive was essentially meaningless. Her middle-class teachers thought they were giving important guidance, but young Donna had learned a different set of lessons.

I have seen this lesson play out in my own work frequently, when my coworkers will get so frustrated with our clients for quitting jobs at the slightest setback—a petty argument with a coworker, perhaps, or a family issue competing for their attention. From a middle-class perspective, impulsively quitting a job can seem crazy! A middle-class job means economic security, career potential, and even a significant part of one's identity and self-worth. Even the minimum wage jobs that many of us had as young people had significance, because our middle-class environments had taught us to expect a career someday. That first job (in my case, cashier at a hardware store) was starting to build a résumé toward that end. However, seen from the perspective of someone who's learned poverty's lessons, quitting a job makes more sense. Poverty teaches that a minimum wage job isn't worth much; that it will likely evaporate sooner or later anyway. Self-respect or family support are much more important since they're more likely to endure anyhow.

Some of the lessons that poverty teaches are more universal, and pierce right to the core of people's sense of self-worth and identity. Beegle explains the often subtle but pervasive way these lessons are taught:

> When was the last time you had to visit your Department of Motor Vehicles for one of the services that couldn't be done in the express line, or get an updated copy of your Social Security card? If you live in a big city, these situations may call for you to take a

number, wait in line for an hour or more, and experience the frustration of not having the correct paperwork so that you need to come back at another time—so you can stand in line for another hour. These offices are generally open from nine to four, not convenient hours for those of us with jobs. For most of us, these "chores" happen infrequently and we endure them.

What would your life be like if most of the services you needed to survive required this kind of take-a-number-and-wait-your-turn, we're-sorry-you-are-not-properly-prepared experiences? Many of the messages we receive about our worth are not communicated directly through verbal communication, but come to us indirectly through nonverbal means, such as the amount of time we have to wait, the tone of voice in which we are addressed, or the look on others' faces as they see how we are dressed. When messages do not fit our self-concept, such as the long wait for the middle class person, we either dismiss them as an anomaly or find a way around the situation. However, if our daily life is full of similar type messages, we tend to take them on as part of our self-concept.[58]

Little daily experiences like having to wait in line, the facial expression of the grocery store clerk when you pay with a voucher, the teasing of your classmates when you're not wearing the right brand, the inevitable comparison of your living situation with that of "normal" families on TV shows, are all tiny little slights that over time can erode the foundation of someone's sense of worth, like drops of water weakening stone. Add to that the much more overt examples of poverty shaming that can frequently be heard from politicians, media, or popular culture,[59] and soon there's a veritable flood of messages of inferiority. This is oppression, and can easily become internalized oppression, when individuals believe these messages and "take them on as part of our self-concept."

Again, lessons learned can be unlearned, and Beegle validates this with her own story of realizing the value of education, reclaiming her personal sense of dignity and self-worth, and learning how to communicate and thrive in a middle-class world with the help of trusted mentors. She also believes that overcoming internalized oppression is enabled by a deeper and more comprehensive knowledge about the true causes of poverty. A comprehensive poverty education is important to people who have experienced oppression and privilege alike.

For instance, Julia Dinsmore tells the story of meeting an Italian sociologist who shared that "she'd never seen a culture blame and shame its poor like we do in America."[60] For her, that insight was utterly transformative. She writes, "Bless you, Ms. Lady Not from Here. You interrupted the daily conversation between my ears that went something like this: *What is wrong with you, Julia? You can't even figure out how to earn income enough to support three sons? You must be doing something terribly wrong!*"[61] When, as individuals and as a society, we begin to understand systemic causes of poverty and systemic influences on individual behavior, then the shaming can relent, and people who have lived under that shame can start to free themselves from it.

More of Donna Beegle's insights on cross-class communication and cooperation will be explored in greater detail later on (See Steps Four and Six). For now, considering the lessons taught by poverty can help allies better understand one another without reverting to judgment and condemnation.

This model can also help allies examine how their own perspective may have been shaped by their class environment, whether it was teaching them these same lessons, or different lessons of middle class or lessons of wealth. For instance, Betsy Leondar-Wright, in her insightful book *Class Matters: Cross-Class Alliance Building for Middle-Class Activists,* identifies six challenges for middle-class allies to overcome based on the lessons they've learned from their class context.[62] They include:

1) Moving from pretense to authenticity

2) Moving from politeness and caution to openness and humor

3) Moving from competition and superiority to confident humility

4) Moving from excessive abstraction to groundedness

5) Moving from guilt to balanced responsibility

6) Moving from individual achievement anxiety to community interdependence

Just like with the lessons that poverty teaches, not every middle-class person will recognize their own experience in this list. But as we do, we can learn from our allies, and begin to move, without guilt or shame, into a place of more "balanced responsibility" for our own learning and self-reflection.

Learning from clients: Walking in each other's oppression

One of the most painful personal lessons I learned about poverty shame came, ironically, from one of the most rewarding experiences I had while working with families experiencing poverty. It was a rare moment of possibility in the poverty industry. The organization I worked for was invited to compete for a grant from a corporate foundation. The grant was unusually open-ended; the company wanted to fund a project that would give job seekers greater skills to be successful in the workplace, and they wanted their employees to be able to participate as volunteers. Within those broad parameters, they were willing to entertain ideas.

The only problem was that our senior leadership was struggling a bit to come up with ideas. Commendably, the directors and development folks within my organization decided to seek the suggestions of front-line staff. So, I offered an idea, they listened, and then suddenly I was very surprised to find myself in the middle of designing a brand new program for the organization.

My peoposal for the grant was based on the conversations I'd had with my clients over the previous five years as I'd talked with them about their career aspirations and interests. Frequently, I heard clients say that they wanted to work "in an office." Some knew exactly what they meant by that, whether they wanted to be accountants or executive assistants or project managers. Others knew only that they wanted a job where they could wear cute outfits and heels instead of non-slip, rubber soled shoes. Either way, working "in an office" was something many desired, but few were able to access.

Long story short, our organization won the grant and I got to spend the next year working with our funder and area employers to design and implement a short-term training program for entry-level office professionals. In that first year, we enrolled 35 parents receiving public assistance, and they had notable successes. A very high percentage found employment after the training and they increased their wages by almost $2.50/hour over their previous employment. We involved business leaders and hiring managers as volunteers in the program so students got networking opportunities and chances to learn alongside middle-class professionals with experience in their field. Finally, one not insignificant success was that African American participants actually did better than the average in terms of employment rates and wages, so we were in a very small way chipping away at Minnesota's drastic racial disparities in unemployment.[63]

Developing that program was one of the highlights of my career so far. I was extremely grateful that my organization gave me the chance to develop my idea and see it through, and I was very proud of meeting all the benchmarks we had set in our original grant proposal. It wasn't all roses, however. Even though the vast majority of participants found employment, not all did. And some were offered jobs that weren't in their desired field, but they took them because survival demanded it. At one point midway through the first year of the program, I was trying to help my most recent cohort of graduates find opportunities when I became very discouraged. I had clients dealing with severe health issues, housing crises, unexpected pregnancies, lack of access to transportation and undiagnosed learning disabilities, and that was all just in one class! I had a student call me pleading for help finding a job, just to no-show to an interview the following week. Even when I offered to drive her to a second job interview, she disappeared.

At the same time as my cohort of students were experiencing such severe challenges, I was also trying to make some big personal decisions that would have wide-ranging impacts on my career and my life. With all this pressure, I started developing rather intense anxiety and insomnia. How was I going to help move my own and my clients' lives forward? Why weren't we achieving greater success?

As I lay awake at night ruminating on the anxiety and frustration I was experiencing, I realized that some of it had to do, in a round-about way, with oppression and poverty shaming. Because I'd been given the opportunity to build this program from the ground up, and because I'd designed it from the knowledge gained from my relationships with participants about what they wanted and needed, I subconsciously started to believe that this could actually be the intervention that could emancipate my clients from poverty. This should do it! This one would be different. I'd teach an amazing four-week training about Microsoft Excel and how to dress to impress. Then all my students should be on a lifelong career path to prosperity.

In retrospect, that was clearly a wildly unrealistic standard of success. That's not to deny that, for some of the participants in the class, they did actually begin a career path to prosperity, or at least freedom from the authoritarian demands of public assistance. But for others, the intertwining causes and effects of their economic circumstances were far too tangled for one little four-week training course to sort out. I should have known that, and if I thought about it dispassionately, I did know that. However, in my heart I was holding on to some unrealistic hopes. I'd subconsciously fallen into the same sort of individualistic fallacy about the causes and solutions to poverty, and this time I applied it to myself. I should be enough. I should teach well enough, network well enough, and motivate my students well enough to overcome their poverty.

A purely individualistic view of the causes of poverty leads to shaming and blaming of the poor for not being able to overcome their poverty. In this case, an individualistic approach led to self-inflicted spillover shame when I was confronted with the reality that I, as an ally, was not enough to overcome my students' poverty. I had internalized the presumption of my own capacity and then I internalized the guilt when I didn't meet my own standard. It was a miserable place to be. But once I came to a deeper understanding of what was going on, I was able to be more forgiving of myself, and slowly the anxiety started to lift.

Before we go on, I want to be very clear that talking about this idea of spillover shame does _not_ mean that I'm advocating for allies to have no accountability, internal or external. If we want to be about the business of ending poverty and working with others in solidarity to do it, we _have to believe_ that eradicating poverty is possible, for each individual and for society. And all of us, people living in poverty, allies with economic privilege, service providers and others have to hold ourselves and each other personally accountable for working toward that aim.

Of course, it won't be easy or quick. Working to end poverty will almost inevitably mean moments of frustration and disillusionment with our ability to create change in our own lives and in society. Indeed sometimes disillusionment is important, because it may be informing us that we need to change course. Other times, though, when frustration and disillusionment turn to shame, it's now a manifestation of our collective oppression. That's when we need our allies to encourage us, help us find hope, and if necessary, call us out on our grandiose assumptions. I had some very patient allies who listened to me and empathized when I was in my moment of despair, and their support was invaluable in helping me process it and bounce back.

I know, now, in my heart that I did some very valuable work by creating and implementing that program. It's work that I am proud of, even if it was not enough to definitively end poverty for every one of those 35 families. That outcome will require the work of many, many more allies working in solidarity against oppression. It will require work that even spans entire societies and cultures, across history and generations, as we will see next.

Maria Yellow Horse Brave Heart: Historical trauma and cultural healing

> *Wherever peoples are being decimated and destroyed, subsequent generations will suffer. We need only heed the traditional American Indian wisdom that, in decisions made today, we must consider the impact on the next seven generations.*
>
> *- Maria Yellow Horse Brave Heart*
> *& Lemyra DeBruyn* [64]

One other model to understand oppression comes from the research of Maria Yellow Horse Brave Heart.[65] She has done extensive work on the concept of historical trauma, which is a way of conceptualizing oppression that I regard highly. Before I expand upon the definition and implications of historical trauma, I should note that Brave Heart's context is the American Indian experience of colonization and genocide, so it is quite different from class oppression. However, I believe there could be parallels to the experiences of families surviving generational poverty. Indeed, the concept of historical trauma has also been applied to many other groups. It originated in scholarly exploration of the Jewish people's experience after the Holocaust, and has also been used to describe the experiences of other indigenous groups, peoples who have experienced war and genocide, and African Americans following slavery in the United States.[66] According to Brave Heart herself, "the crux of our argument has far reaching implications for other colonized, oppressed peoples throughout history and those being oppressed, as we write."[67] I would argue that historical trauma may also be affecting many people living in poverty, even though they are not usually thought of as a people or a culture unto themselves.

Historical trauma begins when a large population or entire culture of people experiences trauma on a massive scale, such as the warfare against and violent displacement of American Indian people by European (and later European American) colonists.[68] The original trauma may be contained to one generation, or it may continue on and on, as was the case for American Indians. The trauma is also usually multi-faceted, including physical, cultural, and psychological threats. Notably, part of the American Indian trauma was the attempt to eliminate Native culture. Language and religious practices were banned. Many children were removed from their homes and raised in boarding schools, where they frequently experienced abuse and were taught nothing of their native culture, language or history.[69]

The attempted destruction of culture is an especially important element, because not only was that traumatic in and of itself, but it also weakened the healing practices of the people. Brave Heart contends that American Indian people experienced, and continue to experience, unresolved grief over the traumas they have suffered.[70] The grief is never processed because, first, the traumas are continuing and perpetuating themselves, and, second, because the cultural practices of expressing grief and healing from it were suppressed. Brave Heart believes that reclaiming cultural and religious knowledge, practice, and pride is essential to move forward from the hurts of the past and seek a more just future for American Indian nations.[71]

What I most appreciate about the idea of historical trauma is that it provides a conceptual bridge between the historical/political and the personal. Historical trauma refutes the false dichotomy between systemic oppression versus individual pathology as the sole causes of human suffering. Instead, unresolved grief explains how individual or family dysfunctions may be directly connected to broader systemic and historical injustices. Brave Heart believes that many of the challenges prevalent among American Indian people today—substance abuse, domestic violence, low educational attainment—are expressions of and continuations of the trauma responses of generations past.[72] She believes that if people do not heal from trauma and unresolved grief, they will almost inevitably respond to it in unhealthy ways, and end up passing on the trauma to current and future generations.

> Present generations of American Indians face repeated traumatic losses of relatives and community members through alcohol-related accidents, homicide and suicide. Domestic violence and child abuse are major concerns among American Indian communities throughout the country. Many times deaths occur frequently, leaving people numb from the last loss as they face the most recent one. These layers of present losses in addition to the major traumas of the past fuel

the anguish, psychological numbing, and destructive coping mechanisms related to disenfranchised grief and historical trauma.[73]

Now this is not absolute. Many people, American Indian or otherwise, have experienced horrible traumas but have drawn on internal and community sources of resilience to heal and to move forward.[74] Many people have transformed their trauma into motivation to make sure that future generations never have to endure the same personal or cultural traumas that they did. But not everyone finds that strength; not all communities are that resilient. On the level of a population or culture, historical trauma is a useful model to help us understand how oppression can become self-perpetuating.[75]

The other thing I like about Maria Yellow Horse Brave Heart's work is that she demonstrates that healing is possible, and grief can be faced and processed in healthier ways. She is a clinician, and has developed approaches to support community health that integrate Lakota cultural and spiritual traditions with standard mental health practices.[76] Other researchers have shown how traditional American Indian practices of oral history and storytelling, even storytelling about traumatic experiences, can build a narrative of resilience and courage that help people achieve psychological strength.[77]

Just like the theory, the clinical practice of addressing historical trauma spans the personal and political. "Community healing along with individual and family healing are necessary to thoroughly address historical unresolved grief and its present manifestations... Without such a commitment to healing the past, we will not be able to address the resultant trauma and prevent the continuation of such atrocities in the present."[78] Recovering from oppression, as individuals, communities and a society, is multidimensional. We need to address the structural inequities of our economic systems, and at the same time help people reclaim their personal and cultural dignity that has been buried under oppression and shame.

Exactly what healing from generational trauma would look like in the context of poverty is yet to be determined. As with the American Indian community, developing such a healing practice is definitely something that should be led by people who have survived and recovered from that trauma themselves. But as allies, we can all draw on the knowledge of historical trauma to better understand how our past experiences, and those of generations before us, may be carrying forward to impact our own well-being.

Identity: Acknowledging our influences and avoiding absolutes

Before we move on from learning about how oppression and privilege operate in our various identities, it's important to clarify a few points about identity, in particular, race. This book is not primarily about race. It is mostly about class. And although it may seem obvious, it deserves to be stated: race and class are not the same thing. There are wealthy people of color whose economic privilege cannot shield them from racism. There are also poor white people whose racial privilege has not propelled them into the middle class. There are quite a lot of them as a matter of fact.[79] This is important for a number of reasons.

One reason is that our public narratives wrongly associate race with class.[80] Pretending that poverty is only a problem for people of color is a way to further stigmatize poor people and to reduce political support for solutions to poverty (due to the racism endemic in our society and political systems). It also adds a whole extra layer of shaming for those people of color who are living in poverty. When I discussed stereotypes and discrimination with my students, I would always point out that the largest number of people in Minnesota receiving welfare benefits were white.[81]   That racial pattern wasn't usually represented in my classroom due to residential distribution, so it was often a big surprise to the people of color in the room. I felt it was important that they knew the facts to contradict the discriminatory narrative.

In addition to stigmatization, conflating race and class often creates barriers against people acknowledging their privilege.[82] It may be hard for a person of color to see their class privilege when they have felt the oppression of racism at work in their lives. Or it may be difficult for a man to acknowledge his gender privilege when he struggles to support himself or his family. Being able to take apart our multi-layered identities is important to being more honest with ourselves about how we've experienced privilege and how we haven't.

At the same time, as human beings we don't exist as distinct, discrete identities. We go through our days as whole people with all those identities swirling around together. As a society we don't make nice neat distinctions, either, between the oppression we inflict based on race versus that based on class versus that based on sexual orientation, etc. It all swirls together and intersects, intentionally or otherwise.

Class oppression, in particular, is intersectional because, as a result of discrimination, almost all other "isms" increase the likelihood that people will experience poverty. [83] People of color are more likely to be poor (proportionally) because of racism. Women are more likely to be poor because of sexism. People with disabilities are more likely to be poor because of ableism. So classism, uniquely, is its own "ism" and an outcome of other "isms." "Class is not just a factor in inequalities of wealth, privilege, and power; it *is* that inequality... Class is the beginning point and end product of all other forms of oppression. It is the essential structure of society, the sum total of all the other inequalities."[84] Poverty, then, is often evidence and essence of other oppressions.

Oppressions not only intersect, but there are also many ways in which they function similarly regardless of toward whom they are directed. For instance, we just looked at the concept of historical trauma, which has been observed in groups as different as American Indians, Jews, and political refugees from various homelands.[85] I argue that it may also be relevant to people living in generational poverty. To some extent, no matter who you are, oppression is oppression, and all oppressions are interrelated. In Anne Bishop's words, "each form of oppression is part of a single complex, interrelated, self-perpetuating system... As long as we who are fighting oppression continue to play the game of competition with one another, all forms of oppression will continue to exist."[86]

Therefore, although it is imperative not to confuse different identities and different oppressions carelessly, it is also necessary to recognize their intersections and similarities. Indeed, throughout the book I will draw from thinkers from many different perspectives, some of whom are more focused on a race analysis or gender analysis than a class one. If I'm translating, I'll be upfront about the fact that I'm doing so, because, as we just said, race and class (and other identity categories) are not the same thing. At the same time, I feel that it's appropriate to move fluidly between viewpoints, because oppressed peoples (or the oppressed intersecting portions of our swirled up identities) have a lot to learn from one another. That is part of the idea of solidarity after all.

Finally, as we conclude, it will be beneficial to recognize once again that none of us are (or should be) completely defined by our oppressions or our privileges. For one thing, we are multi-dimensional human beings, not just identities. We have personalities; we live in families and communities and cultures that have many elements beyond just their experiences of oppression or privilege. For another, even our communal experiences of oppression and hardship sometimes have some unintended positive consequences. For example, William Cross asserts that, although Christianity was imposed on African slaves against their will, they eventually embraced and reinterpreted that religious tradition.[87] African American Christianity remains a powerful personal and cultural influence. Arguably the Civil Rights movement and many other examples of African American resilience and resistance are rooted in that strong religious tradition. Oppression is never "good," but human beings have a remarkable way of adapting in the face of adversity and in some cases developing new strengths and qualities that they may never have otherwise.

We have all been shaped by our environments, in some constructive ways and in some less than constructive ways. As Paulo Freire would say, we all bear the marks of our origins. As Donna Beegle would say, we have learned lessons from our class experiences. As Maria Yellow Horse Brave Heart would say, we carry the unresolved griefs of generations past. The good news is that as mature human beings, we can assess those influences, celebrate the positive ones and challenge the destructive. We can achieve *conscientização*. It is a slow and always incomplete process. Freire was right to say that we must re-examine ourselves constantly. But the reward of our careful examination is personal and social liberation from shame and mistrust—well worth the effort.

Step 3: Explore How Internalized Oppression or Privilege May Affect You

Internalized oppression or privilege may affect your behavior in cross-class relationships. For example, sometimes people who have internalized privilege believe that due to their education and experience, their ideas and suggestions will always be superior to people who have less education. They may begin to think of people in poverty as less intelligent or less informed, and not consider their ideas seriously. This may happen at an unconscious level, even though the person consciously believes that everyone's ideas are important.

If an ally is experiencing a confusing conflict with people from a different class background, the ally should first consider whether internalized oppression or privilege might be contributing to the conflict.

Like many things, oppression and privilege are obvious, once you start to notice them. Until you do, you'll be limited by blind spots and assumptions.

I'll never forget one occasion when I ran headlong into someone's blind spot—someone who probably thought of herself as an ally to people experiencing poverty. I was looking into graduate school programs, and I visited a school which offered a Master's in Public Policy. This school was very highly regarded in the field, and spoke all the right language of social change and commitment to economic justice. I was very curious about their program. So, I took the tour, sat in on a class, had lunch with a current student—the whole production. Incidentally, the class session was about a financial asset building tool for low wealth families. I was as knowledgeable about it as the graduate students in the class, because a guest speaker had just presented such a program to my students a week earlier.

After the class, I spoke with the professor. I asked her if she ever invited people from the community to speak to her classes or help educate students in the program. She wavered a bit, said they sometimes did, but then admitted that it was rather challenging to arrange. Anyway, she said, they had lots of information about communities in poverty, so it wasn't worth the effort to try to find an individual to come "just to put a face on the data."

I was floored. Just to put a face on the data?!? The people I knew who were living in poverty—my students, the partners in the Allyship Project, my mentors—were so much more than faces on the data. Shouldn't they be a part of the conversation about poverty policy, and not just subjects for study?

Of course, those were the kinds of retorts and questions I thought of well after I had left campus. I will admit that in the moment I didn't challenge the professor about her dismissive words, so I was not a very good ally—to her, or to my allies, the people with whom I had actual relationships. I hope that today I'd be more assertive. But at least I was able to recognize the classism of her statement and its incongruence with the stated mission and aims of the school. The whole experience also helped me demystify advanced education. It helped me realize that while a graduate degree would be one way to learn,

I was also learning an amazing amount from actual people. I was learning directly from people who struggled with and survived poverty every day. The lessons they taught me were important, too, as much as the lessons from the "experts" with their data sets.

That particular "expert" whom I talked to that day had internalized a certain degree of her privilege as a (presumably) upper middle-class, highly educated, white professional. She had internalized a patronizing attitude toward people in poverty, even while teaching in an institution dedicated to social justice. She's not alone. As Betsy Leondar-Wright points out, "Middle-class activists in the US have a proud history of initiating, organizing, and supporting movements for progressive social change. We also have a not-so-proud history of overlooking potential allies from other classes, failing to come through for movements led by poor and working-class people and stepping on the toes of coalition partners through classist assumptions."[88] Even "progressive" values don't shield us from learning prejudices.

We've all been exposed to many messages about our own worth or lack thereof, and when we start to internalize those messages and believe them (consciously or unconsciously), it can poison our worldview and our behavior. Those of us who internalize privilege may start to see ourselves as inherently more worthy or capable. Those of us who internalize oppression may start to see ourselves as inherently flawed. We can internalize assumptions and stereotypes about others as well, until we get to the point where, without even realizing it, we've dictated who gets to make decisions and have opinions, and who only gets to be a data point.

Before we proceed any farther in the discussion of internalized oppression and privilege, I'd like to offer a few words of caution. If you're anything like me, you'll find the whole phenomenon of internalization fascinating. Or maybe that's just my particular geekiness. I studied psychology in college, and I loved exploring the workings of the human mind. But I had seriously considered majoring in sociology instead, or a blend of the two disciplines, because I am actually most captivated by the intersections between the social and the personal. My favorite class in my whole college experience was my senior seminar, called Lives in Context. It was my favorite not only because that was the class for which Julia Dinsmore presented, but because in that class we delved into how our most personal experiences and perspectives are shaped by social forces and interrelations. We talked a lot about various kinds of oppression and how they can be internalized at the most micro level. I found it captivating.

As a psychology major, I also took an introductory level class on psychological disorders. During that class, as anyone else who has taken it probably experienced, I developed a case of "Psych Student Syndrome." When you catch a bad case of P.S.S., abruptly you and everyone around you seems eminently diagnosable with one disorder or another. Every little twitch and quirk of human personality suddenly seems like a sure sign of a serious pathology. It can be unsettling. Thankfully, most psychology students get over their P.S.S. and learn with time to be more discriminating. They manage to temper their urge to diagnose everything.

The parallel to our current discussion is the challenge to avoid "oppression student syndrome." While seeking to learn about oppression and privilege and their internalization, we must resist the temptation to pathologize and diagnose our allies at every turn. We should especially be careful about diagnosing our allies who have experienced poverty, assuming that every little twitch and quirk is a sign of internalized oppression. People in poverty already get pathologized enough. Over the years they've endured analyses of everything from their lack of moral fortitude, to their toxic culture of poverty, to exposure to trauma.[89] Allies don't need to contribute to that.

Internalized oppression and privilege are real, and should be addressed and contested. Sometimes, we may even be able to help out a fellow ally by constructively pointing out a bias or blind spot coming from their internalized privilege or oppression, like I might have been able to do if I'd had a wittier comeback for the professor. But honestly, those kinds of challenges are usually only going to be productive once we've established a deep trusting relationship and built a history of solidarity. And even then we should still avoid a sophomoric over-emphasis on "diagnosing" others. Some people turn "allyship" into a sport of judging political correctness. Whoever can identify the most internalized privilege wins! This tends to shut down authentic relationships, not foster them. It also is usually a distraction from careful consideration of <u>one's own</u> internalized oppressions. Cura te ipsum: Physician heal thyself. As we strive to work in solidarity with others, we should seek self-awareness on how our own internalized oppression and/or privilege may be affecting us. I will share a little story about an ally who helped me gain some clarity on this very subject.

The internalized oppression diagram

Early on in my conceptualization of the Allyship Project, I sought some advice from an ally who had facilitated a good training on poverty. We were talking about the process of oppression and its internalization, and in the course of our conversation created a diagram of sorts. It was no work of art, just a hasty scribble, but nevertheless it artfully helped me discover an important truth.

The diagram had two people (stick figures), one representing people in poverty, and one representing people from privilege. There was also a building with a (rudimentary) bell tower, representing institutional powers like schools, government and business. Then we had a series of arrows. One arrow pointed from the building to the person in poverty,

Figure 1. Internalized oppression diagram.

representing systemic oppression. The unfortunate stick figure in poverty internalized this oppression and began to fulfill its prophecies, acting in ways that confirmed the stereotypes of the middle-class stick figure. This was represented by the second arrow from the oppressed stick figure to the privileged one. Finally, the privileged stick figure, now wearing glasses to help it observe and judge those in poverty, asserted its privilege by designing and maintaining the systems of power, the final arrow.

This diagram evolved because I was struggling to explain my intentions in wanting to investigate allyship. I knew I was curious about oppression and how it impacted the ability of people to work in cross-class coalitions. But I wasn't explaining that well, and my mentor thought I was wanting to explore only how oppression was internalized by those who experienced it, and how that distorted <u>their</u> ability to combat poverty. She was deeply skeptical that I could truly understand that process, not having experienced it myself. My ally had grown up in poverty, although she was now economically in the middle class, working professionally with many well-intentioned but poorly informed service providers. She didn't really want one more middle-class armchair theorist telling people in poverty how they needed to change to overcome their internalized oppression.

Her challenge to my plan was enormously helpful, because it clarified that I was in fact most interested in a missing arrow in our diagram. I didn't want to tell stick figures in poverty how to change, I wanted to tell the stick figure from the middle class how to adjust those glasses. I wanted to help the middle-class stick figure better understand its own internalized privilege, and overcome it to develop more effective relationships. I wanted to draw a new arrow from the privileged stick figure to the oppressed one, an arrow of non-judgmental perception and recognition of common humanity. I wanted an arrow that shattered myths and skewered stereotypes, and opened up a path for both stick figures to advance on the bell-tower building together to change institutional powers and patterns.

Figure 2. Revised diagram of mutuality and solidarity.

When I was finally able to articulate that and my ally understood me, she got very excited. Instead of invasively trying to describe and influence others' experiences, I was seeking to describe and influence my own, and then share that with others like me who had experienced the same sort of class privilege as I had. That was something different, and much more appropriate in her view.

For allies from privilege, it is a little too easy to develop a morbid fascination with internalized oppression and to focus on how people in poverty should overcome it. Constantly trying to change people in poverty is a knee-jerk reaction that comes from our culturally ingrained individualized view of the cause of poverty—a blame the victim approach. While I certainly don't believe that oppressed people should have to live with the lies of oppression constantly weighing on their consciousness, I'm still grappling with the question of whether there is a role for privileged allies to play in the healing of internalized oppression, or if that is work oppressed people must do for themselves. In either case, I do believe that those of us with privilege should focus on healing ourselves first, to make sure that we can be truly present and effective in our relationships with all our allies.

The affliction of the affluent: Internalized privilege

For those of us who grew up in the middle or owning classes, we have most likely been affected by some internalization of our privilege. Internalized privilege can manifest itself in many, many ways. Not all of these effects are negative. As I implied in my own story of my upbringing and education, some of the privileges I received, like positive attention from my teachers and being nominated to leadership positions from a very young age, helped me be confident in my own intelligence and capacity for leadership. This is not a bad thing. Indeed, the destruction of confidence is one of the most insidious effects of internalized oppression. Anytime we can raise confident kids we should celebrate that.

The problem comes when those positive influences are taken too far or are misattributed. Social psychology research has shown that individuals, especially those from Western, individualistic cultures, tend to be self-serving when attributing the reasons for particular outcomes.[90] We assume that successful outcomes are the result of our own internal characteristics—our capacity, effort, and tenacity. Conversely, we tend to attribute unsatisfactory outcomes in our lives to situational factors. So the raise is due to hard work, but the layoff is due to economic difficulties. A car accident is due to the weather, but getting to a destination safely is due to good driving skills. Obviously, this bias doesn't hold true 100% of the time, but it does influence our perception of situations. If we extend this theory to a societal level, we can see how this self-serving bias could take on a class dimension, as people who benefit from economic privilege tend to disproportionately attribute their success to internal factors.

Many people take these self-serving tendencies even further when observing the behavior of others. Another principle of social psychology is the "fundamental attribution error," which states that in this society we are more likely to attribute the behavior of others (positive or negative) to their personality or intentions than we are to take situational influences into account. [91] So someone acting aggressively must be an aggressive person. Someone acting confidently must be capable at what they're doing. Someone being inconsiderate must have intended to be so. Interestingly, we are less likely to fall for this error when assessing our own behavior, as we're more aware of the context of our own actions than that of others.[92] However, when it comes to others, we rarely invest the mental effort to imagine or learn the complete context, instead preferring to make casual assumptions. The class implications of this are obvious. As we've already discussed Americans are quite likely to blame people in poverty for character deficiencies and moral failings.

To review, the self-serving bias means we tend to think we created our successes with our own effort or skill, but see our failures as caused by circumstance. But when it comes to others, the fundamental attribution error says we see their behavior as a direct result of personality or choice. Combining the two, we are likely to attribute our own successes to our internal strengths, and the failures of others to their internal faults. Quite the recipe for class-biased judgment.

Allies from economic privilege can work to counteract these biases by intentionally concentrating on the countervailing influences. This means trying to understand how our own successes were influenced by external privileges and societal patterns. It also means understanding how the challenges of others are influenced by their context. That, of course, brings us back to learning about poverty directly from people who have experienced it. In general, stories are far more effective than statistics in helping us understand the "why" behind the "what." Stories assist us to identify human commonalities that break down our biases and assumptions.

Sometimes our own situational influences are invisible until we are confronted with someone who had a different situation. For instance, Donna Beegle talks about her amazement when she learned about the lives of middle-class people who had lived in one house their entire childhood, who had quiet spaces to do their homework, who had never had family members become the victims of violence or incarceration.[93] She said this was transformational because she saw the environmental advantage of others (their class privilege) for the first time. As she says, "I thought everybody had the same kind of life I did—they just handled it better." For allies from privilege, learning these kinds of details about other people's circumstances can help us let go of the same internalized assumption—that we just handle things better.

One of the biggest flashpoints of internalized privilege comes around education. Sadly, class has now become one of the biggest determinants of an individual's likelihood to access higher education.[94] So that means that cross-class relationships will very often include a disparity in education. This can have a lot of implications, both interpersonal and practical. In my experience, my college education was fundamentally about teaching me and my peers to communicate. In the process we were socialized to assume that somebody would be interested in whatever we had to say! Someone would respond to our comments, would read our papers, and even if they disagreed they would take our ideas seriously.

This can lead to an internalized sense of importance. As we've discussed, a confidence in one's own importance is not always a bad thing, but it can get out of proportion. A highly-educated ally can easily end up unintentionally dominating discussions and imposing their ideas and plans in cross-class situations. Familiar with talking and being listened to, privileged allies can take up all the air in the room. Later on in Steps Five and Six, I'll discuss strategies for privileged allies to both check their privilege to avoid dominating conversations in cross-class situations, and to use their privilege to open up new perspectives in conversations that are not inclusive by class, but probably should be. For now, we will continue to practice identifying our internalized privilege.

Another way that internalized privilege can manifest itself is in assumptions about resources. Middle-class folks like me tend to have pretty reliable access to basic resources. We often assume that others do too. So we may host an event at a location with free parking, but not think to check the bus schedule or offer car pools for those without access to a vehicle. We may schedule meetings at times convenient for working professionals (who can participate in social change work as a part of their paid profession), but not think about working people with unpredictable hours. We may assume that our allies will always be able to check email or voicemail or even have a working phone, and we may get frustrated when they're "not responsive."

Donna Beegle describes living in generational poverty as living in crisis, all the time.[95] If we think back to a time that we were in crisis, after the death of a loved one, during a natural disaster, or in the grips of a health scare, we can remember how that situation monopolized our resources. All our mental energy, all our time, and a lot of our tangible resources got redirected from the normal routine to deal with the critical needs. Crisis is exhausting.

People tend to have great sympathy for one another when the cause of a crisis is visible and acute. But when the crisis is poverty, on-going, onerous, and sometimes hard to see or understand, some of the sympathy can be missing. Without other information to contradict our self-serving assumptions, we start to think that everyone has our life. They just don't handle it as well.

A good thought experiment for an ally from economic privilege is to try to imagine what a person in poverty might be required to go through just to participate in the ally relationship, whether that relationship takes place during a meeting or social event or class. What was the situation in their life and in their home as they started their day and figured out how to allocate their time? Who else depended on them for help that day? Kids, family members, neighbors, others? What transportation did they use to get to the event? How easy was that and how long did it take? What other resources did they need to participate? Food, papers, communication devices, money? How easy was it to access those resources and maintain them? What else is competing for their mental and emotional attention? By asking these kinds of questions, we can develop greater consideration of what we're asking from one another. We can also then get some ideas about how to offer helpful assistance without putting our allies in the awkward position of having to counter our assumptions just to ask for something.

Within the Allyship Project, we tried to be as attentive as possible to these sorts of resource issues. Our group always met in the evening at a central location with public transportation. For those who couldn't access their own transportation, public or otherwise, we carpooled. Our sponsoring organization, A Minnesota Without Poverty, provided funds that covered food at our meetings and stipends for our members to help defray any of their costs such as childcare. It wasn't a perfect solution. There were still some differences of opinion about how stipends should be handled. And admittedly for me, who was organizing the meals and the gas cards and all the rest, it was a lot of work. But at least we were trying to make sure that participating in the Allyship Project didn't place an undue burden on anyone.

Class privilege manifests itself in countless ways, large and small. And as we've seen, those of us who have it are often blithely unaware of it. Sometimes, though, class privilege will be asserted and defended, often in surprising or contradictory ways. Next, I'd like to share a story about when a student of mine proclaimed class privilege as a matter of self-defense. I believe this incident has deep implications for the sometimes counterintuitive ways that internalized privilege and oppression confront and interact with one another.

Learning from clients: "I'm not poor"

As a trainer, I have facilitated a great number of discussions with my clients about race and class and how these social forces have impacted their personal experience in life and job search. I must admit I was initially a little nervous about having these conversations. I was well aware that I was white, middle-class, childless, and college educated, all of which could be points of difference with my students and potential barriers to honest conversation. I imagined nightmare scenarios of people yelling at me or each other, complaining to my boss, or getting so traumatized they'd withdraw from my class. Nonetheless, I thought the issues were too important to just ignore, so I made it a part of my curriculum and entered into the conversations as sensitively as I could.

None of my disaster scenarios ever happened. For the most part my students seemed eager to talk, were very considerate of me and each other, and shared honest but respectful reflections. In fact, far from nightmares, we often had fascinating and enlightening conversations. Sometimes students from different cultural or religious backgrounds even got some insight into others' experiences that they might not have gotten otherwise.

There was only one time that a conversation on stereotypes turned a little tense, and the source of the tension caught me completely by surprise. The discussion had started routinely enough. To introduce the topic of stereotypes, I used an activity I had once experienced in a diversity training. I identified a category of people and then asked the class to name stereotypes about that group, whether or not they believed them to be true. (Actually, I encouraged students to give each other the benefit of the doubt and assume that others did <u>not</u> believe whatever stereotypes they stated.) I always started with stereotypes about blonde women. Since nine times out of ten I was the only blonde in the room, it was a non-threatening and usually funny way to introduce the exercise.

But then I would ask the class to identify stereotypes about welfare recipients. It never took long to get a full list of vitriol and misrepresentations. Next, I would work with the class to debunk some of the stereotypes, and then I would usually turn the conversation to how they resisted the influence of such negative messages directed against themselves and their families. This time, though, things took a different turn.

One of the members of the class was reflecting on how she felt about the list of stereotypes. She shared that they were difficult words to read, even though she knew they were untrue. As a caveat, she said, "I know they're not true, except maybe 'poor.' That's pretty true." Objectively, it was true about everyone in that room except me. As welfare recipients, every person there was from a household below the federal poverty line.

However, the class erupted. "I'm not poor!" "Uh, uh!" "Poor is living in a cardboard box without enough to eat. I put a roof over my children's head, and they always eat. My children aren't poor!"

I don't entirely remember how I responded to the class discussion that day. I'd like to think that I brilliantly helped demystify the judgment and assumptions elicited by the word "poor," and helped all the members of the class see that their worth as human beings was not equal to their financial worth. (One of Julia Dinsmore's favorite lines is "My IQ is not equal to my income.") Unfortunately, I doubt I handled it that gracefully. I was honestly quite shocked at the class's response. "Really?" I thought to myself. "You don't think you're poor? You're on welfare, for heaven's sake!" So through my puzzlement I tried the best I could to let people share their honest thoughts without reverting to any personal attacks on each other.

Ironically, I learned later that the woman who was most insistent that she wasn't poor because she wasn't living in a cardboard box, had only recently been living in a shelter for the homeless. From an outsider's perspective, she had been about as close as one can get to having to sleep on the streets, which might, presumably, have caused her to have more empathy and solidarity with the "poor." But from her perspective, she had never actually crossed that threshold. Furthermore, she was in a shelter because she had made sacrifices to move to a new city that she hoped would provide greater opportunity and safety for her family, even if it meant living in a shelter for a time. She had sacrificed privacy, family support, and pride to, as she said, keep a roof over her kid's heads. Now, paradoxically, her sacrifice of pride was itself a new source of pride and one of the few she had left. No, she wasn't about to admit to being "poor."

This discussion stayed with me for a long time as I pondered the implications. First, it revealed to me a deeper level of the danger of internalized oppression than I had realized before. I saw in that classroom how internalized oppression could become a barrier to solidarity, even between people who, from a distance, seemed to be in nearly identical circumstances. Because society has attached such shame to the idea of being "poor," my students—who were, objectively, poor—were resisting the label.[96] They were preserving some sense of dignity by comparing and distancing themselves from others who had it marginally worse than they. Brené Brown believes this is very predictable. "Most of us buy into the myth that it's a long fall from 'I'm better than you' to 'I'm not good enough'— but the truth is that these are two sides of the same coin... We don't compare when we're feeling good about ourselves; we look for what's good in others. When we practice self-compassion, we are compassionate toward others. Self-righteousness is just the armor of self-loathing."[97]

We human beings have a persistent habit of comparing ourselves to others, which can either feed our insecurities to "keep up with the Jones,'" or bolster fragile egos by helping us feel at least a little bit superior.[98] Research indicates that higher degrees of inequality in a society make us even more attuned to markers of status differences, more anxious about our own place in the social standing, and more willing to go to extreme lengths of denigrating others or even resorting to violence to fend off any threats to our self-worth.[99]

I applaud my client for doing what it took to provide for her kids in the best way she had access to at the time. I have seen how people in poverty, especially parents and caregivers, often have to go to extreme lengths to provide basic necessities for their children. (Anyone who thinks that poor people are lazy has probably never had to wait in line for two hours at a food shelf and then walk back to a shelter through dangerous neighborhoods with bags of heavy cans.) So I respect my client and others like her for making sacrifices for her kids. But it saddens me that, in order to find her self-respect, she had to assert superiority over someone else and employ the very same stereotypes that the rest of the world would likely have directed at her and her family.

I also began thinking about how this temptation to compare ourselves favorably with those "below" us in the social strata might play out for someone like me with more relative privilege. Specifically, I thought about someone who, like me and my family, experienced temporary situational poverty. Donna Beegle defines situational poverty as a temporary hardship usually precipitated by a life crisis (divorce, health issue, etc.) that afflicts people from an otherwise middle-class context.[100] Situational poverty can be a severe shock for those of us who suddenly lose the economic security we had previously taken for granted. When our internalized privilege has taught us that our economic success is due to our personal strengths and wise choices, poverty, even temporary, can be a bitter pill to swallow. Interestingly, the woman in my class who started the whole controversy by admitting that she felt "poor" seemed to be in situational poverty. She was one of the few white women in the class and had lived a more comfortable lifestyle prior to a divorce. She was feeling acutely "poor."

However, middle-class people in situational poverty often still retain some of the privileges of their former circumstances. For example, situational poverty doesn't reduce one's education or knowledge of middle-class norms in the workplace, so finding employment can be marginally easier. Even if someone experiences as dire a situation as losing their house and having to sleep in a car, this is only possible because they still have a car. People experiencing situational poverty might also still have a network of friends or family who can assist with resources or connections. That was certainly the case in my family's experience. Our network generously shared their resources to help us find housing and help my parents find employment. So while situational poverty can certainly be painful, it is by definition temporary. And most people experiencing it retain some privileges that help ensure that it is temporary.

Once it's over, we can get back to the business of assessing our self-worth in light of new experiences. Perhaps surprisingly, people who have lived most of their lives with economic privilege may actually have an easier time being open about having experienced temporary poverty. Remember our self-serving attribution biases, which help us attribute negative outcomes to situations rather than our own behavior.[101] We might be able to point to a divorce, or an illness, or an economic shift to explain our temporary poverty. Also, in hindsight, it's easier to remember one's success in getting out of poverty than the discouragement and disappointment of falling into it in the first place (those self-serving biases again).

Moreover, we've already talked about how internalized oppression tends to occur as the cumulative effect of millions of tiny interactions—subtle facial expressions or brief spiteful phrases that erode our self-concept one millimeter at a time. For most of us who have experienced situational poverty, as acutely painful as it may be at the time, it doesn't have the same long term corrosive effect as poverty that has lasted a lifetime or even many generations. The result? Once our income bounces back, our self-concept bounces back relatively quickly as well.

Then, ironically, rather than denying any solidarity with "poor" people, we may claim too much. By this I mean that someone who has experienced situational poverty may be quite willing to admit their poverty, and presume they now have had the same type of experience as someone who has suffered economic oppression for generations. Rather than developing true empathy, situational poverty can lead some people to be even more unaware of their internalized privilege. As Beegle describes, a formerly poor middle-class person can sometimes be the harshest critic of people in poverty.[102] I made it out, after all. Why can't others?

Clearly, we <u>all</u> have work to do to understand our own internalizations and guard against the impulse to make ourselves feel better by judging others. Even those in generational poverty are not immune from stereotypes about themselves. And for the temporarily poor, situational poverty does not negate privilege. Finally, those who have always experienced the security of wealth may have nothing but stereotypes with which to understand people from other circumstances. Paolo Freire says we are all socialized to idolize the oppressor and disparage the oppressed by virtue of being a part of an oppressive society.[103] None of us have the privilege of avoiding that.

Before we delve more deeply into more of Freire's thoughts, I want to briefly explore one more topic that came up for me after the "I'm not poor" conversation in my classroom. That topic is language. I have been a part of social movements and organizations that sought to end "poverty" and had the word "poverty" in their goals, their mission statements, their very name. All these organizations claimed to desire more involvement and participation from people living in poverty. But if the very people who we were seeking to involve refused to see themselves in that label, how can we expect them to want to participate in an organization named after it?

I am honestly not sure of the best response to this. Historically, there have certainly been instances where oppressed groups have taken a label imposed upon them and reclaimed it into a source of positive identity and power.[104] Perhaps if Dr. King had been alive to continue the work he started on the "Poor People's Campaign" right before he was assassinated, [105] we might have seen the word "poor" take on different meaning. As it is, if a word still carries shame and stigma, we must be careful how we use it or ask people to identify themselves with it.

At the same time, I believe it's also important to be clear and use bold language. Sometimes initiatives will try to describe their goals with more positive terms. So instead of fighting poverty, they're promoting prosperity or equality or economic justice. Most of the time, this sort of rebranding feels like a euphemism to me. In my opinion, words like "prosperity" or "opportunity" are so vague that initiatives in their name risk being co-opted into milder reforms that don't actually address the interests and needs of the most oppressed. So, until I can come across better language, I will continue to talk about my work as fighting against poverty and economic inequality, although I will try to be more sensitive about how those words might label and stigmatize people.

Idolization of the oppressor and cultural invasion

We've acknowledged that we all have a tendency to compare ourselves against those with less privilege in an attempt to make ourselves feel at least a little bit superior. But we also have a tendency to look up. We look to our "superiors," or those society has judged to be so, and often want to emulate them. Our culture teaches us to idolize the rich. Through TV shows and lavish magazine spreads, we learn of the cheap thrills (albeit very expensive cheap thrills) of being rich—the houses, the cars, the clothes, the vacations, the parties. It appears to be a much better life, lived by much better people, than our own. Paulo Freire teaches that in an oppressive social context, the "model of humanity"[106] is to be an oppressor, since the oppressors are the only people who seem to have independence of thought and action within that social context.

Freire states that identifying with the oppressor is not the best course of action, for a few reasons. First of all, he argues that being an oppressor is actually a dehumanizing situation in its own right. "The oppressors do not perceive their monopoly on *having more* as a privilege which dehumanizes others and themselves. They cannot see that, in the egoistic pursuit of *having* as a possessing class, they suffocate in their own possessions and no longer *are*; they merely *have*" (emphasis in original).[107] Freire contends that the obsession with having starts to extend beyond possessions to other humans.[108] Other human beings, and everything else around one, become things to control or have. This distorted sense of privilege and power is not the true meaning of human potential or relationship.

Nor is it even very satisfying. The wealthy may <u>have</u> houses, cars, clothes, vacations and parties. But research shows us that the enjoyment of these things is shallow and fleeting.[109] When comparing internationally, happiness is, in fact, correlated with average income, just about up to the point where your needs are assured and then perhaps a little more for a few indulgences and security. That amounts to about $25,000 a year in US dollars. Beyond that? No significant gains in happiness as income increases. Bummer.

The other danger of idolizing the oppressors is that, in an effort to gain economic security and move out of poverty, individuals may start perpetuating the kinds of injustices that lead to poverty in the first place. Freire observes: "It is a rare peasant who, once "promoted" to overseer, does not become more of a tyrant towards his former comrades than the owner himself. This is because the context of the peasant's situation, that is, oppression, remains unchanged. In this example, the overseer, in order to make sure of his job, must be as tough as the owner—and more so."[110]

What does this mean in an economic context without a lot of peasants or landowners? Simply that in our efforts to eradicate poverty and help individuals escape from it, we shouldn't seek to replicate some of the less desirable parts of economic privilege like materialism or exploitation. This is not to say that negative cultural patterns like materialism are solely practices of the economically privileged. To the contrary, the "context of our situation" can make this seem desirable to all.[111] As bell hooks writes, "tragically, the well-off and the poor are often united in capitalist culture by their shared obsession with consumption. Oftentimes the poor are more addicted to excess because they are the more vulnerable to all the powerful messages in media and in our lives in general which suggest that the only way out of class shame is conspicuous consumption."[112]

Regardless of who is the "more addicted," American materialism is a pretty universal expression of our idolization of the oppressor. Even so, it can lead to recurrent clashes between people of different economic situations. It's almost a cultural caricature that people in poverty may not be able to pay their rent, but they'll have a big screen TV among their possessions when they get evicted. Or if it's not the TV, people with economic privilege will often find something else to criticize about poor people's spending habits: clothing, cigarettes, sugary beverages, you name it.[113] Why, they wonder, would someone with significant economic hardship waste their money on such "luxuries?"

Donna Beegle has some good thinking on this type of situation, and she actually draws on the work of Freire.[114] Our culture teaches us that we need certain possessions and status symbols in order to belong. So people in poverty are often trying to purchase much more than meets the eye when they're purchasing "luxuries"—they're trying to purchase social access and normalcy. Plus, one of the lessons that poverty teaches is that money and material goods may sometimes come but they will always eventually get taken away. So the idea of saving money toward a future goal is fruitless. Far better to enjoy the immediate indulgence, since that will be taken away at some point in the future too.

As we see, it is not only the oppressors who seek to have. However, those of us with privilege certainly tend to have a lot more, sometimes to the point of amassing credit card debt and other risky behaviors. And we're more likely to preach the benefits of having, from social status to economic expansion. This is a practice that Freire terms "cultural invasion."[115] The oppressors of a society will impose their cultural values onto all, forcefully or shrewdly, to try to further encourage identification with the oppressor. Cultural invasion can manifest itself in many ways, and we'll talk much further about how allies can resist it in Step Six.

Essentially, Freire believes that resistance is possible and critical to achieving a greater degree of humanity for everyone—oppressor and oppressed. He believes that people in poverty, the oppressed, will not achieve their liberation simply by joining the ranks of the economically privileged—in effect, becoming oppressors. Instead, he believes that human liberation requires creating a new, more just economic situation for everyone. "Liberation is thus a childbirth, and a painful one..., the labor which brings into the world this new being: no longer oppressor nor longer oppressed, but human in the process of achieving freedom."[116] By challenging our internalized admiration for the oppressor, we can find a new model of humanity that supersedes oppression.

Spotting the invisible: Becoming more attuned to internalizations

In the upcoming chapter, we will turn our discussion toward working with people, and veer away from the more self-focused topics we've explored thus far. But before we do, I would be remiss not to say that learning to recognize internalized privilege and oppression is both essential to being a good ally, and woefully insufficient. One of the most pointed criticisms of "allies" (those of us who seek to be, or who claim "ally" status but often don't live up to the term) is that we often spend all our time and energy in self-reflection and in identifying our and others' privilege. As Mia McKenzie states, "Acknowledging your privilege is all the rage these days. The fact is, though, when you acknowledge your privilege you've done exactly zero things to combat oppression... Naval gazing about your privilege is just another way to centralize your privileged self while simultaneously taking no action in the fight against oppression, thus ensuring that oppression continues as usual. It is not enough to acknowledge your privilege. You must actively push back against it."[117]

At the same time, McKenzie states that the first thing to do to combat inequality is to educate yourself on the realities of oppression.[118] So please consider deeply what has been explored so far. And, then, please keep reading and start connecting with other potential allies to take action together. Being a true ally is about being in relationships, and it's in the course of those relationships that our assumptions are challenged. It's in relationship that we learn about other people's experiences and the situations that have impacted their lives and their choices. It's in relationship that we can appreciate our unique strengths and our shortcomings, and develop teamwork that can capitalize on the former and compensate for the latter. It's in relationship that we can create new models of human society that don't depend on the dehumanizing oppression of any human being by another.

Internalized privilege and oppression put up barriers to these authentic relationships, but paradoxically internalizations are also best challenged by authentic relationships. So the key is to enter into relationships with gratitude and humility—gratitude that our allies will put up with us, and humility to learn from others, even when what we learn contradicts our self-serving biases.

Step 4: Seek out Opportunities to be in Relationship

Look for opportunities to be in mutually beneficial relationships with people from a different class background than yourself. Look for opportunities where people are working together on a common goal, and power and leadership is shared. Find and appreciate "bridge people" who have authentic connections in multiple communities and can help make introductions and facilitate relationship building. These should be relationships other than service provider/client, donor/recipient, or advocate/victim.

Intentionally, seeking opportunities for relationship is the fourth step in our journey toward allyship, not the first. This may seem surprising, given that relationship is such a pivotal part of the Allyship Project's definition of an ally. As you may recall, our definition is:

> *An ally is a person who seeks to end poverty, and who partners with people from all class backgrounds to work toward that goal.*
>
> *An ally develops personal, responsible, respectful and mutually beneficial <u>relationships</u> with people from*

different class backgrounds than him/herself. These relationships are not necessarily friendships, but are at least respectful working relationships bound together by a common goal of ending poverty.

So if relationships are so primary, wouldn't we expect them to be the first step toward implementing allyship? After all, one <u>cannot be</u> an ally in isolation. It is a fundamentally relational word. If you are an ally, you are an ally <u>with</u> someone. If you operate in solidarity, you are in solidarity <u>with</u> a person or a group. Even supporting the cause on one's own is not sufficient to be an ally. As we heard in Freire's words, "a real humanist can be identified more by his trust in the people which engages him in their struggle, than by a thousand actions in their favor without that trust."[119] Action is great, but trusting relationships are essential.

Nonetheless, diving too quickly into relationship is not the best way to practice allyship. As we've been discussing in Steps One through Three, there is a lot of internal reflective work which is a very helpful precursor to being in an allyship relationship. We've seen that most of us are mis-educated or uninformed about the realities of other people's class-based experiences. Those of us with internalized privilege are likely to enter into relationships with an exaggerated confidence in the value of our own ideas, and a habit of leading and directing everything. And those of us with internalized oppression are likely to suffer from some degree of imposed cultural shame, and perhaps an undue deference or nervousness about speaking up for ourselves. So, deeply engaging in internal reflection about our own class experiences and how they've shaped our expectations is a way to be considerate of those with whom we will subsequently be in relationship.

Self-examination is much more than navel gazing. Doing our reflective work may help us avoid some of the classist blunders that can come from well-intentioned but uneducated allies. Or at least an allyship education can help us recognize our classist blunders for what they are when they inevitably occur, and find ways to apologize and recover.[120] If we take some time to begin to heal from our class-based injuries and influences, we will be more prepared to create and maintain healthier cross-class relationships.

This is not to over-complicate allyship relationships. Fundamentally, cross-class relationships are just human relationships. Though it seems obvious, this is actually a critical point. If we only ever attend to the identity dimension of our relationships, we can easily miss the human dimension of them, and the human dimensions of our allies. Joan Ostrove and Gina Oliva make this point in their discussion about deaf/hearing allyship:

> This sense of 'accept me with this particular identity (or identities) but don't focus on it to the point that you cannot see my other human characteristics' begs for an overt awareness that the member of the subordinate group (in a cross-identity relationship) is just as human, just as uniquely complex, and just as valuable as the member of the dominant group—and is, therefore, worthy to be a friend, colleague, ally or partner.[121]

Most of what it takes to build good cross-class relationships is what it takes to build any human relationship: be considerate and respectful of others, show up in a genuine and honest way, be open to learning about someone else's life with humility and curiosity. Thankfully, we humans are naturally relational creatures and therefore already have a lot of capacity to work in solidarity. We can go a long way just by treating one another with basic decency.

Cross class relationships do have a few unique characteristics, though, starting with how rarely they occur. This was one of the disheartening, though inescapable, themes of the research I did into allyship. I heard about how rare true solidarity is from the members of the Allyship Project. I also heard it during a number of follow up interviews I did to supplement our work as a group. I interviewed people whom I or members of the Allyship Project knew and admired as good allies in one way or another. Most worked in professional helping positions: a public aid lawyer, a professor, a couple leaders in social service organizations, a student activist. As professionals, they lived in relatively middle-class circumstances, although their class experiences growing up had ranged from working class to owning class. These were all individuals who did personal and professional work to combat poverty. They had been commended as people who truly sought to work in solidarity with those in poverty. So I was confident they'd be good resources for my project.

Everyone with whom I spoke did contribute valuable insights and stories. But there was also a universal experience of confusion at some point in every interview. There would be a moment of nervous laughter and uncertainty, and then the person would confess that they weren't really sure they had been a part of enough authentic allyship relationships to confidently speak to the experience. Everyone agreed solidarity was a desirable goal, and many talked about <u>attempts</u> to build cross-class initiatives or relationships. But no one, even among these dedicated and reflective social change makers, immediately identified with the experience of cross-class allyship as a regular part of their everyday work.

I found this terribly sad. It speaks to the deep divisions and distance between different groups in our society. It also speaks to how rarely institutions are set up to actively invite, encourage, and enable the meaningful participation of oppressed people. In the experience of those I interviewed, even advocacy or educational organizations focused on social change tend to be run by educated, paid professionals who rarely have had personal experiences with poverty. And although those leaders may sincerely desire the involvement of people living in poverty, limited resources, limited time, limited personal networks and, sometimes, limited allyship competency make it unlikely.

Consequently, as we discuss the topic of building relationships across class, whether individually or between groups, we will start by exploring contexts where they are more likely to actually occur—within non-profit service or advocacy organizations. We will then address other contexts where it may be possible to create cross-class relationships that more fully reflect our ideal definition of solidarity: *relationships other than service provider/client, donor/ recipient, or advocate/victim.* Throughout the chapter, the focus will be on building and sustaining those relationships in a responsible, respectful and mutually beneficial way.

Then, in the next chapter, we will explore what kinds of social change initiatives allies may actually undertake with one another, and how to share leadership while defining and implementing those common goals. Hopefully, this conversation will be beneficial for those lucky enough to already find themselves a part of a functioning allyship network or organization, or for those who desire to build one or evolve an existing organization into a more inclusive space.

Trying to be an ally in the non-profit industrial complex

For many non-profit organizations, a key component of their mission is serving individuals and families struggling with generational poverty. Other non-profits have a mission focused on health or education or civil rights, for instance, but find that poverty intersects their issue area and that they disproportionately serve the same clientele. In all these contexts, sometimes the relationships developed between service providers and their clients are wonderful, helpful and live-giving. Other times they're not. As allies, how can we push service providers to live up to their name and truly serve the best interests of families in poverty?

Part of Donna Beegle's work involves helping service organizations develop a greater poverty competency. She teaches service professionals to be "poverty coaches" and then to take their knowledge back to the organizations in which they work to spearhead change. She gives many examples of what a poverty competent organization might look like, primarily drawn from her extensive experience working with teachers and school districts.[122] For instance, she encourages schools to think about how they welcome students and set the tone at the beginning of the day, especially for students who are late. Poverty competent schools recognize the frequent level of crisis among families in poverty and the inconsistent access to resources like transportation, which may result in more frequent tardiness. Schools can reframe a punitive approach to "tardiness" into an encouraging approach that welcomes students and expresses appreciation that they have come to school, regardless of the time of day.

Beegle also asks, "What is homework if you don't have a home?"[123] She encourages schools to assume that learning will only realistically happen in the school environment, where there is quiet space, climate control, and adults who aren't experiencing crisis who can provide support to students. As a matter of policy, then, a poverty competent school will provide safe environments for after-school learning and will not expect additional work to be done at "home." Other examples of poverty competency include collaborating with other organizations to provide comprehensive services, and taking a whole family approach that addresses the needs of parents, children, and anyone else significant in the family environment.

As I trained with Beegle to become a poverty coach, I found the concept of poverty competency inspiring, but a little daunting. Implementing these kinds of changes would be hard enough in a school system. Many of the recommended practices of poverty competency would inevitably collide head-on with some educators' concepts of fairness or how to encourage personal responsibility (worthy values even if not the most poverty-informed). In my own professional context— a workforce development organization—there were even additional barriers to implementing poverty competency practices. Our mission as an employment agency was to prepare people for employment, and most places of employment are what Beegle would call a "mono-economic" environment,[124] the very opposite of poverty competent. A mono-economic institution assumes that everyone has access to similar levels of resources, or even if they don't, they should be held to the same standard of behavior out of fairness. This is despite the fact that, as Beegle points out, "it is not 'fair' to treat people who have unequal resources equally."[125]

A mono-economic attitude sets up people in poverty for conflict in the workplace. Think about typical flashpoints of employer-employee relations. Punctuality and attendance. Ability to disregard obnoxious or insulting behavior from customers or coworkers. Following a dress code. Time management. All of these can be directly impacted by the material realities of poverty or the lessons that poverty teaches.[126] According to Beegle's theories and my own observations, individuals from poverty often experience the following frictions in the workplace:

- Punctuality and attendance: Chaotic life circumstances are likely to lead to competing demands on a worker's time. In addition, poverty teaches that caring for your family is more important than a job since the job is likely to fall apart sooner or later anyway.

- Dealing with insults: Poverty teaches that environments can be hostile and dangerous, and you had better respond immediately to personal threats or risk being taken advantage of. Poverty also teaches that social systems designed to protect people (courts, police, etc.) may not work to the advantage of people in poverty, so you are on your own to defend yourself, physically if necessary.

- Dress code: Limited resources mean that a person in poverty may not have access to the expected apparel or grooming. Also, conforming to certain middle-class "professional" standards of dress and appearance may be alienating in certain social environments.

- Time management: Poverty teaches that planning ahead is futile. Also, people in poverty have rarely seen any evidence of the truism that hard work leads to success. More often, hard work just leads to more work, but the same inadequate pay check.

To repeat a note of caution before we go on, these "lessons that poverty teaches" are not absolute. Not every individual will respond to their environment in the same way, and not every individual living in generational poverty is experiencing the same environment. That said, I saw the above workplace dynamics play out many, many times in the lives of the individuals with whom I worked. As I developed greater poverty knowledge myself, I was able to better understand the reasons behind the behaviors I observed.

But I still struggled to determine how my personal knowledge should impact the practice and policies of my work. At the organizational level, what was the best way to respond? If my colleagues and I allowed ourselves to be more lenient on certain requirements in an effort to exercise poverty competency, were we actually preparing our clients for the realities of the mono-economic workplace? After all, employers were unlikely to change their expectations. They would still require all of their employees to be on time, demonstrate patience, follow the dress code, and work efficiently. Would we do our clients a disservice if we did not expect the same?

Cross-class relationships in social service settings are rife with these kinds of conundrums, with no easy answers. I never found a full resolution to this issue myself. I personally tended toward leniency on all kinds of things, although I would be very direct with my clients that employers were not likely to be as flexible. However, I had coworkers who genuinely disagreed with me, and favored a "tough love" approach. It is not an easy thing to achieve (or even to agree on) poverty competency.

The limits of poverty competency

As contentious as it may be, if social service providers developed greater poverty competency, the families in generational poverty receiving services from these organizations would certainly benefit. But even a poverty competent organization is not necessarily an allyship organization. When issues like homework policies or late arrival policies are discussed, there is almost never any client input or shared decision making. Often, the best case scenario is input from staff who experienced poverty in the past (if they're willing to be open about those experiences with their coworkers). The more frequent case is that middle-class professionals set the rules, or at least decide to what extent to enforce the rules, based on their own understanding and values of what's "best" for their clients. Social service providers exercise a lot of power over their clients in poverty, often making decisions and discretions that will determine access to basic needs. This kind of power imbalance makes it nearly impossible to develop true, cooperative, collaborative relationships rooted in solidarity.

Social service and advocacy organizations can also have mixed incentives, as Julia Dinsmore taught me when I first heard her name the "poverty industry," or more broadly the non-profit industrial complex. [127] Like most other creatures, the poverty industry has an instinct for self-preservation. Sometimes this can come into direct conflict with the interests of the individuals who are supposedly being served. A few years ago, when the Minnesota State Legislature was considering an increase in the minimum wage, there were some nonprofits who came out against it because it would limit the number of individuals they could employ in sheltered employment.[128] Whose interests were really served by paying people with disabilities or welfare recipients a wage far below a living wage? What was the broader goal: building a bigger client base for the organization, or moving people out of poverty? As another example, I distinctly remember a conversation at A Minnesota Without Poverty where someone pointed out that on the way to ending poverty, we would need more food shelves, but once we got there we would need none. It is a poignant truth, because few food shelf Executive Directors would embrace eventual obsolescence in their strategic plan.

Beyond self-preservation, there are often broader political forces and compromises reflected in social service policies. For instance, the welfare system that employed me could be seen as a safety net for the country's most vulnerable citizens—poor children. Or it could be interpreted as corporate welfare subsidizing the inadequate wages companies pay to their "disposable" workforce.[129] Does welfare ultimately serve the interests of needy children, or mega-moguls? To my estimation, it does both at the same time—an optical illusion of political expediency. Unless we can see both aspects of the illusion, we will be unable to make informed decisions about how best to support our allies.

The non-profit industrial complex leaves much to be desired, then. It is not much of an ally to its clients in poverty when it leaves them out of leadership and decision making. And the poverty industry will always have a hard time earnestly advocating for the end of poverty when its business model necessitates it to continue. But, until we need none of it, we may need more. And would-be allies will almost certainly interact with the non-profit industrial complex in one capacity or another, as clients, as staff, as volunteers, as donors, as board members. So how can we bring an allyship ethic into non-allyship contexts?

We can begin by looking for ways to encourage poverty competency within our organizations. That means, firstly, educating ourselves about poverty as we've already outlined. It also means interrogating our assumptions about fairness, remembering that "it is not 'fair' to treat people who have unequal resources equally."[130] Next, we can encourage more legitimate input from allies who have lived or are living in poverty. This may come in the form of inviting clients or constituents to participate in governing bodies or encouraging the diversification of staff. It is wonderful when staff closely represent the clientele they serve with regard to race, gender, age, and, especially, class background. When making hiring decisions, it is important to consider personal experience and capacity for empathy as valuable assets of a potential employee, like fluency in a language or a degree. It should not be the only consideration when hiring, but a significant one.

We will discuss more deeply in the upcoming Step Five how to support the leadership of people living in poverty. For now, suffice it to say that these kinds of efforts toward inclusivity and solidarity may take some very significant investments of time and money on the part of service or advocacy organizations. People living in poverty may need material support and/or education to be prepared to take on decision making or staff roles. As a modest example, you may recall in Step Three we discussed how our Allyship Project provided stipends, transportation, and meals to make participation practical for the members of the group living in poverty.

Also, leaders experiencing poverty will certainly need emotional support from their allies. One case in point: for a number of years, I served on a board tasked with addressing racial disparities in employment in the city of Minneapolis. One of my allies once told me just how taxing these meetings were for her. Being a person of color herself and having received welfare benefits in the past, the disparities and adversities the board discussed were not theoretical for her. They were very real, very painful, lived experiences for herself and many in her family and community. So, as the mostly white, middle-class professionals and bureaucrats talked and talked and talked, she prayed and prayed and prayed. Prayer was the only thing that made those dry, detached and analytical meetings emotionally tolerable. This ally's passion and urgency were instrumental in ensuring that the group accomplished anything more than empty talk, but her contribution took an emotional and spiritual toll.

Finally, for those of us receiving services from or working in the poverty industry, one of the best things we can do is keep a healthy perspective. We know the poverty industry alone will not solve poverty. We need to supplement the work we do providing service, or the work demanded to receive services, by collaborating with our allies to advocate to make the poverty industry extinct.

We must also remember that our role in the poverty industry is not our role as human beings. As recipients of aid, we cannot let receiving assistance dehumanize us. As practitioners in the poverty industry, we cannot let giving assistance be our only entrée to our humanity. As I shared in Step Two, I occasionally got reminded of this the hard way, when I got so wrapped up in defining myself as a "helper" that I started to experience spillover shame when my "help" wasn't enough to eliminate poverty for the families I worked with.

Allies can make important contributions within the poverty industry, especially when they push to make it more poverty competent. But it's not the only way, or even the most important way, to work in solidarity with others toward a more humane system.

Don't burn your bridges: Finding and valuing bridge allies

If getting a job or volunteering in the poverty industry to "help" others isn't an express route to allyship relationships, then how do we get there? Since most of us live our lives increasingly segregated by economic class,[131] how do we even find people from backgrounds other than our own who desire to partner to create change?

For some of us, this question can be a perplexing puzzle. But for others, interacting with people from different backgrounds isn't an enigma; it's an everyday reality. Because class can be mutable over the lifespan, many people have lived in more than one class environment at different times in their lives. They may continue to move between multiple "worlds" as they maintain relationships from those environments. Other people may have experienced primarily one class context themselves, but due to family or deep social connections, they know many people from other backgrounds. I call these folks "bridge allies," and the diversity of experience and network that they have is extremely valuable.

It should be noted that not everyone who has lived in more than one class circumstance is a bridge ally. First of all, as we've noted earlier, many people who have lived otherwise middle-class lives experience short-term situational poverty at some point. While this can lead to a greater degree of empathy and understanding for people living in poverty (or it can occasionally lead to an even harsher, more judgmental attitude, as we explored in Step Three), situational poverty is not the same thing as living in a different class environment. People in situational poverty usually maintain the same social and family connections with other middle-class people.[132] They may live in the same types of neighborhoods, attend the same schools, and keep the same associations that they did before, or, even if they don't, the change is usually fairly temporary. In my family's case, although we temporarily couldn't afford our own housing, we were never actually without a place to stay. Until our church helped us rent a modest house, we "house-sat" for friends on vacation. So although I'm sure "house-sitting" was extremely stressful and disruptive for my parents, the actual spaces in which we stayed were probably nicer than anything we'd ever been able to afford!

Other people do experience a more substantial class repositioning, but still may not choose to be bridge allies. Many first-generation college students, for example, grew up in generational or working class poverty. They often feel a profound cultural shift when they enter predominantly middle class or wealthy college environments.[133] Many immigrant families also experience dramatic class mobility, either upward or downward, as they adjust to a new culture and economic system that may present great challenges or afford them great opportunity. But not all of these people choose to become bridge people. Some deal with the changes by trying to fully acculturate and "fit in" to their new class identity, and may not want to be reminded of former circumstances. They may be all too happy to leave behind their old lives as targets of shaming and scapegoating.

Others remain engaged in both their new and former identities, but move between them divergently like a bilingual person switches languages. (Sometimes, navigating multiple class identities involves literally switching languages, or at least expression patterns. Both Linda Stout and Donna Beegle talk about the process of learning to communicate in "middle class."[134] More about communication patterns in Step Six.) For these bi-class-lingual individuals, it may be too confusing to try to overlap languages. Blending communities could leave them feeling awkward and alienated in both identities. Indeed, many people who have experienced class mobility are afraid of ending up much like a bridge—stretched between two points but no longer truly a part of either.

So, while we should exercise compassion for those who choose not to be bridge allies, we should be in awe and gratitude of those who do. True bridge people maintain relationships in multiple communities and they find ways to bring them together. They often serve as cultural translators—helping people understand and empathize with those who have had different experiences. They can help challenge mono-economic assumptions, and because they do so from within groups their challenges can sometimes be accepted more easily. Bridge people can be amazing allies, and they can help bring allies together who otherwise might never have met or recognized their common purpose.

A great first step, then, toward building authentic allyship relationships and coalitions is to recognize bridge allies and ask for their help. After meeting Julia Dinsmore during my last year of college, I stayed in touch, and later asked her directly to be a mentor. In my professional life, when I heard about a woman in a partner organization who was interested in racial justice (and whose clients raved about her as a case manager), I invited her out for coffee to learn more about her work. When A Minnesota Without Poverty hosted a training or a poetry slam or a study group that involved people living in poverty, I went. In all of these ways, I found amazing bridge people who became allies, and who deeply enriched my life and my work. And when a bridge ally whom I trusted did me the honor of introducing me to someone else, I always tried to follow through on building that relationship.

As I've said, bridge allies are amazing resources who should be cherished. Unfortunately, they're often taken advantage of. So as you seek bridge allies, here are a few ways to show your respect:

- Recognize the fatigue of bridging.

   As we've discussed, being a bridge ally takes a lot of effort in balancing multiple identities. Bridge allies often end up in the uncomfortable position of having to challenge many of the people around them about their cultural insensitivities. It can be exhausting to constantly be called upon to help people recognize their ingrained assumptions or potentially harmful actions, especially since not everyone is always happy to receive that help. So bridge allies need to be supported, and appreciated for their contributions. Also, as their allies, we shouldn't let our feelings get hurt if bridge allies need to take a break, or even decline projects/relationships to maintain their own energy and wellbeing. [135]

- Strive for mutuality.

I have no doubt that many of my bridge allies have contributed far more to me than I could ever repay. But that doesn't mean I haven't tried to find ways to support their work, emotionally, actively, and at times financially. For bridge allies living in poverty, in particular, it is important to recognize that they are often called upon to assist individuals or organizations in ways that, in other contexts, would be compensated highly. They often become psychological counselors, diversity trainers, organizational effectiveness experts, fundraisers, market researchers or translators. And they're often asked to do this work for free, or to "give back" to an organization that has provided them some service. Many bridge allies continue to give generously of their time, talents and relationships because the work matters to them, but as their allies, we should recognize the value of their contributions and try to compensate in any ways we can. We don't want to reduce every allyship relationship to a financial transaction, but I've seen many instances where middle-class professionals were getting a paycheck for their social change work while their allies in poverty weren't. If anything, the reverse should be more common.

- Don't pass the buck.

Finally, allies should continue to take responsibility for developing their own allyship relationships, even while partnering with their bridge allies. I've seen organizations seek to diversify themselves by class or race, until a bridge person is identified to help. Suddenly diversity becomes their problem. Developing cross-class relationships and working in solidarity is everyone's problem (or, really, opportunity). We are all responsible for effective allyship, starting with the personal self-analysis we covered in the beginning of this book, moving into developing organizational poverty competency, and finally welcoming, supporting, and integrating people of diverse class backgrounds into every aspect of an organization's work, especially leadership, as we will discuss in more detail shortly. We all need to be active in reaching out and going to meet people from other class backgrounds. It is not sufficient to simply ask bridge allies to invite people from their networks into allyship relationships, without making the necessary preparations or being willing to leave our comfort zone. If all of us haven't prepared to be good allies, then we've set everyone up for a potentially negative experience, and we may cost our bridge ally important credibility within their community.

That last point bears repeating. If we don't help our bridge allies and the people they know have a good experience, we may not always get another chance. They may not want to come back. Given that, as a society, we tend to be so sequestered with people who've had very similar life experiences to ours, it can be a little nerve-wracking to be invited to a group where nearly everyone else has had a different life experience. I know I've felt that little tingle of apprehension in many different situations—when my African American roommate invited me to an event at a Black fraternity, when I had to network professionally with a roomful of wealthy and prestigious business leaders, when I was travelling to a country where I didn't speak the language... I felt like the odd one out. Sometimes our class differences can be similarly discomforting. So when we ask our bridge allies to bring their friends and families into unfamiliar circles, we can be asking a lot.

Now, just like with the social situations above where I was invited into a new milieu, allyship relationships also invite everyone involved to have enriching experiences that can help us understand other perspectives and build our compassion and tolerance for one another. And if allies are coming together toward a common purpose of improving society, all the more strength is to be gained from diverse relationships. So let's support our bridge allies, work with them to build strong and enduring bridges, and sometimes take the initiative to venture out across them ourselves.

Being fair in the midst of unfairness

As we start to expand our networks and meet new potential allies, we can begin to work toward *personal, responsible, respectful and mutually beneficial relationships,* as described in our definition of allyship. In cross-class relationships, or indeed any other kind of productive relationship, this will require trust. And one of the stickiest complications to building trusting relationships will be issues around money and other resources. This is a touchy subject, but essential to address.

Cross-class allyship relationships take place in the context of an unfair economic system and by definition they're going to include an unfair disparity of resources. Thus, it is nearly inevitable that money will become a source of tension at one time or another in an allyship relationship between individuals or groups with different needs and imbalanced access to resources. I wish I could say that I had all the answers for exactly how to address money and resource issues and treat everyone in allyship relationships fairly, in a way that deserves and maintains trust and mutuality. But, I don't. I do hope to at least narrow the gray areas within which to grapple with this issue.

A good place to begin is to recognize that most of us have a fair amount of ego wrapped up in money. Our culture teaches that earning money is something to be proud of, while being given money due to need is something to be ashamed of. (Oddly, inheriting money is seen as different than being given money; apparently the "worthiness" of past generations' hard work carries forward with the dollars.[136]) So those of us who've had the privilege to access well-paying jobs or other sources of income often take a great deal of pride in our paychecks. Access to income is a privilege, and then the income itself can become one more source of internalized privilege.

Sharing money taps into ego dynamics as well. Those of us with money often want to share it, both out of a sense of fairness and out of the personal satisfaction we derive from doing so. But sharing money can also set up a sense of obligation. It can be a way to control someone or to make them feel inferior, whether that's the intention or not. As Freire taught, there can be a false generosity of *noblesse oblige*, which demands gratitude but keeps the structures in place that produced the poverty in the first place.[137]

I should also note that the willingness to share money can sometimes be in opposite proportion to the amount one has to share. Julia Dinsmore has often said, "If you need someone to lend you money, ask a poor person." Within communities struggling with poverty there is often a much more generous culture of sharing, in part because people recognize that an opportunity for reciprocity will probably come soon enough.

Having said that, allies with economic privilege have access to greater resources, so their decisions about whether and how to share them make a significant impact. My personal belief is that an ally should put their money where their mouth is. If we recognize that our economic system has created an unfair distribution of resources, then we should do our part to voluntarily re-distribute those resources. Further, we should do so, as much as possible, matter-of-factly without creating obligation or embarrassment for our allies. There are many ways to do this, of course, from personal gifts to donations to organizations. When I am sharing my resources, I try to follow a few principals.

First, when possible I prefer to share money directly with allies in poverty to support particular work. This most definitely does not mean that I manufacture "chores" for my allies to do, as if they were earning their "allowance." Instead it means that I seek to support the social change work that they are already doing, much like I seek organizations that do good work in the community and give them my charitable contributions. Social change allies living in poverty don't always have institutional backing, so they may not get a traditional paycheck for their social change work. I think of my contributions as a way to partially make up for that lack of paycheck. Also, if I do ask an ally in poverty to do some significant work for me, then I would always try to offer money or other resources in return.

Second, I try to be compassionate of urgent needs while still maintaining my boundaries. So I help out when asked, but not to the point of putting myself at great financial risk. I, of course, have my own financial needs and priorities. And, like wearing an oxygen mask on an airplane, I believe I can be more helpful to my allies in the long run if I maintain my own financial stability. That also means I spend some money on personal indulgences that I believe enhance my quality of life and help me maintain balance to stay energized for my social justice work. I certainly admire the heroes who vow poverty to serve the poor, but I'll admit I'm not willing to be that saintly. I do try to live simply, though, so that I can be more generous with my time and resources. In the gray area somewhere between the lifestyles of Mother Theresa and Andrew Carnegie, I try to find a good balance, although I'm sure I never get it entirely right.

Third, I try to leverage outside resources to support my allies in poverty. This is an important way to both use my privilege and teach other people and organizations how to have greater poverty competency. For instance, when I first invited Julia Dinsmore to Macalester to speak, I requested money from multiple academic departments and student groups so we could put together a decent honorarium for her. The school regularly pays dignitaries and experts significant amounts for speeches and convocations, but might not have expected to pay a less "prestigious" speaker. Still, I felt that Julia contributed more to my education than others with many more letters behind their names, so I thought she deserved to be compensated equitably.

Finally, I am thoughtful about how I might profit financially from my allyship work. I've chosen to decline to earn money for my work around allyship. In the few instances where I've received paid speaking invitations, I've shared those with members of the Allyship group. I've left the Allyship Project off my résumé so I'm not claiming it as a part of my professional qualifications. And I intend to donate any money made from this book. This has been a personal choice, and I recognize it is a personal choice enabled by my privilege to earn my income from other sources. I do not begrudge anyone who wants to earn a fair living for social change work. However, for me personally, I've felt more comfortable keeping this work removed from any financial motivation.

As an ally with economic privilege, these principles have, for the most part, helped me address financial disparities without either feeling exploited or exploitative. Still, I'm sure there have been times when I didn't draw the line in the right place— when I might have been able to do more to assist my allies or do it differently. It is heart wrenching when allies have acute needs that I cannot meet. But rather than letting myself get swamped with guilt or putting my own financial stability at too much risk, I try to channel that sorrow into motivation for the work we do together.

For allies living in poverty, they also have decisions to make about receiving or asking for resources. Anyone who has survived in poverty for any length of time has had to develop strategies to secure the resources they need. Members of the Allyship Project called this the "survival hustle." Hustles vary—from accessing social services, to entrepreneurial ventures (sometimes legal, sometimes not), to seeking resources from friends and family. Sometimes survival hustles have to get pretty creative, and sometimes they start to move toward manipulative. Unmet needs can push people to take advantage of others in ways they might not want to if it weren't necessary.

It's important not to be too judgmental about survival hustles. After all, for someone with an MBA or a JD, these same hustling skills would be called negotiation skills and command a six-figure salary! However, in general, my allies and I are seeking a less cut-throat world than that. The truth is that survival hustles are not usually a pleasant thing for the parties on either end of the bargain, and they're not very conducive to trusting allyship relationships. One possible solution is to, rather than turning the survival hustle on one another, work in solidarity to turn the survival hustle on institutions with money and power. Combining the access of allies with privilege and the savvy of allies without it can make a formidable partnership to pursue resources that can support the needs of those in poverty.

One final thing for allies in poverty to watch out for is the possibility of getting "pimped" by the poverty industry, as Julia would say. For example, most charitable organizations will have some kind of event, at least annually, where they will share the stories of some of their clients in an effort to raise donations or sympathy. Sometimes these events can be opportunities to celebrate the successes of individuals who have achieved wonderful things, often in the face of great obstacles. And sometimes these events can be degrading displays that reduce people to their neediness. Usually, they're a confusing mix of both. In any case, it's not unusual for someone's touching personal story to raise millions of dollars for an organization whose professional staff get steady paychecks, while the individual who laid their heart bare may still be struggling tremendously. In one instance, a member of our Allyship Project spoke at a fundraiser for a multi-million dollar housing initiative. The fundraiser was an amazing success, the project was built, and yet the speaker remained homeless. She could not get anyone in the organization to respond to her inquiries about benefiting from the homes she had helped to build.

Allies in poverty have a right to demand their fair share for the work they do and the contributions they bring. All allies, especially those with privilege, should support one another in such claims. And although thus far we have discussed mostly monetary resources, an ally's fair share may not always be financial. Often allies will find many other ways to support one another, and they should strive for fairness in those circumstances as well, as we turn to next.

Learning from clients: Be careful what you promise

Friends often do favors for one another, whether it's helping move a couch or introducing someone to a professional contact. These are generous and lovely gestures of friendship, and generally much appreciated by the recipient. Within allyship relationships, doing occasional favors for others is also a generous and lovely gesture, as long as there is an opportunity for some level of reciprocity.

One thing that is important to remember, however, is that for someone living in poverty, a "favor" may be much more than just a favor. It may be a vital resource of huge importance. If someone in poverty needs to move a couch, they don't have the option to hire movers to help. They probably don't even have the option to rent a vehicle to move the couch themselves, as they likely don't have a credit card or available cash for a deposit. And they certainly don't have the resources to replace the couch. So a favor to help move that couch is the difference between having furniture or not—a comfy place to sit which as likely as not will also become a place to sleep at some point for a friend or family member in need.

The lesson to be learned for allies is to be very thoughtful about what you promise, or even what you suggest you <u>might</u> be able to do for someone, because you may leave your ally in a very tight spot if you can't follow through. People in poverty have to deal with a highly unpredictable environment already. When will the landlord stop being flexible about when the rent is paid? When will the car stop running? When will violence break out in the neighborhood? When will the food shelf run low on supplies, or change its policies? When will the kids get sick and will the boss allow time off to care for them? The level of unpredictability and the resulting need to constantly adapt would drive most middle or owning-class people bananas! The stress caused by unpredictable environments and institutions is taxing, so as allies we should not be adding to one another's stressors.

Working in the poverty industry, I did sometimes add to my clients' stressors due to the fickleness of human service systems. Once, I got totally blindsided by a policy change and it was one of my worst days on the job. I was working for a program that provided paid internships for low-income parents receiving welfare benefits. The jobs were temporary and paid minimum wage, but they were jobs. In many cases they led to permanent job offers or résumé enhancing experience that helped people secure other employment. Moreover, the country was in the middle of the Great Recession and even a temporary minimum-wage job started looking pretty good as the unemployment rate was spiking.

As a result of the economic conditions, the agency I worked for and others like it had received extra funds through the federal "stimulus" spending, and we were expecting more. The need in the community was great, but we were getting resources to help address it. I was working as fast as I could to enroll participants and prepare them for internships. Until I got some bad news. Some of the stimulus funding we'd been anticipating was not going to come through. Why? Who knows? Something had changed deep in the layers of inscrutable bureaucracy. Or our agency's leadership had gotten ahead of themselves in the first place. Or perhaps it was some combination of the two. Whatever the reason, the outcome was that I had 35 families on my "pending" list to whom I'd promised jobs that they were never going to get.

Making those 35 phone calls was one of the worst tasks I'd ever been given. What made it even worse was the resignation in the voices of the people I called. I would have almost rather that they cursed and vented. Well, if truth be told, I didn't actually want anyone to take out their anger on me, and I'm sure part of why they didn't was that they heard the genuine disappointment and frustration in my own voice. But I would have understood if they had been angry at me. This was awful! It was unfair and unprofessional, and I was deeply embarrassed to be representing an organization that hadn't taken steps to prevent it.

Nonetheless, for most of my participants, it was just one more time that they'd been disappointed at the whim of the system. It had happened before and it would happen again. Donna Beegle actually identifies this as one of the lessons that poverty teaches. Life is so unpredictable, resources are so unreliable, that planning ahead is futile.[138] This is an important point. People in poverty have been criticized over and over again for a lack of long-term thinking, or inability to delay gratification, or gaps in executive functioning skills, or whatever the latest vocabulary is to describe their planning deficits. At times this has even been "diagnosed" as an actual personality disorder, believe it or not.[139] Interventions often include instruction in goal setting or financial planning or time management. (I myself have taught all of the above as parts of a broader curriculum.) As an alternative, though, perhaps as allies we can develop a more sympathetic understanding of why someone might not choose to exercise or fully develop long-term planning skills in such an erratic environment as the crisis of poverty. And we can recognize the remarkable adaptability, resilience and creative problem solving skills that people do develop to cope.

Also, hopefully, as allies, we can avoid disappointing each other so frequently that the reaction is just weary resignation. We should hold ourselves and one another accountable to only promise what we can actually deliver, and to follow through on what we promise. We should be optimistic but realistic at the same time. By this I mean that part of our practice as allies should be to dream and vision in solidarity together, but we should be very explicit about what are our mutual hopes and dreams versus what we can realistically expect from one another in the short term.

On a related note, when we want to do a favor for our allies, we should make sure we ask permission first. Sometimes our attempts to help may hurt. I'm not talking about the overblown dependency argument here—I'm talking about actual harm as a direct consequence. Let me share an example. Say you visit an ally in her home, and notice that there are some issues with the building that the landlord should be attending to, but isn't. Perhaps they are serious issues like a toilet not working. As an ally, you might be tempted to get right on the phone with that landlord and give him a piece of your privileged mind. Or maybe you know someone at the mayor's office who should get involved. Or maybe your journalist friend could do an investigative piece about shoddy landlords making money off of low-income people.

Those all may be appropriate responses and good ways to utilize your privilege on behalf of your allies, if, and only if, you have their permission and collaboration. Because what you may not know is that your ally has a friend who just left an abusive relationship. That friend is currently sleeping on the couch, which means the apartment is over its occupancy limit. The landlord may be turning a blind eye to the situation. Now, that landlord, just to be clear, really should fix the toilet, but if you bring down the weight of public opinion and city hall in an attempt to make him do it, he may be more inclined to call up an eviction notice than to call a plumber.

Since people in poverty often have to interact with so many powerful systems, they may often find themselves in situations of double jeopardy. Trying to assert their rights (or an ally asserting rights on their behalf) may bring unintended consequences and further struggle.   Systems sometimes retaliate against people who don't cooperate. Even if it is a privileged ally who isn't cooperating, it is likely the less privileged ally who will bear the consequences.

That doesn't mean that allies need to be "wannabe wimps" who just wait around until they are told how to be helpful.[140] Not at all. You can look for ways to be helpful. Just ask before you pick up the phone or write a letter to the editor. Just make sure you can be there to follow through on whatever you've offered to do, for as long as it takes to see it through. Finally, if you say you're going to help move a couch, just show up and do it.

Porch sitting: Enjoying our allyship relationships

Much of this chapter has been focused on ways that allies can try to avoid taking advantage of one another or hurting one another out of ignorance while building relationships. Although important to consider these things carefully, it's also a little dour. As Julia Dinsmore would say, "This work of ending poverty is too serious not to have a little fun!"

Julia has always brought song and poetry and humor into every gathering, even when the purpose of the meeting is to discuss some of the weightiest burdens that human beings bear. She is also a master storyteller, and uses personal and engaging stories to convey hard truths in ways that are relatable and impactful... and funny. In her book, she tells stories of using humor as a community health "intervention," telling jokes and sharing laughter with neighbors who couldn't afford more costly (but not necessarily more effective) therapies.[141] Julia is a wonderful model of how we can bring our whole selves into our allyship relationships, including our human creativity, whimsy and playfulness.

When Julia was raising her children in a tough south Minneapolis neighborhood, and just starting to get involved in education and social change work, she would invite students who were interested in learning from her to come sit on her porch. These "porch sitting" sessions were educational as sure as anything that ever happened in a university classroom. Julia would answer questions and tell stories and help her mentees open up to new perspectives on the world. But unlike the ivory tower, porch sitting took place in the middle of the rest of life, watching the ebb and flow of neighbors moving throughout their days, getting interrupted by children when they needed a snack.

Porch sitting is a lovely way to build relationships and learn from one another. It's social and builds inter-cultural and inter-generational community right in the context of everyday life. It's relaxed and un-presumptuous—no one has to clean their house or make a meal because we're just sitting on the porch. And it's just a casual, fun way to spend time together.

Porch sitting also requires us to leave our established patterns and go meet our allies where they are to spend some time on their front porch. It requires us to break our habits of isolation. So many of us Americans have gotten very used to driving alone in air conditioned vehicles into attached garages where we can go directly into our air conditioned houses and keep the windows and doors sealed against our neighbors. By contrast, porches are from a time when, not having such "luxuries," neighborhoods were more social places and outdoor spaces were shared. It is well worth reclaiming some of that sense of community and intentionally building it with our allies.

The work of ending poverty is too serious not to have a little fun. So let's enjoy one another. Let's hang out on the porch, drink something refreshing, play with the kids, and learn about one another's lives. Let's sing together and laugh together and be fully human with one another. And from the front porch, we'll begin building bridges that will connect us to a better society.

Step 5: Support the Leadership of People who have Lived or Are Living in Poverty

Due to social and economic oppression, people in poverty are rarely given positions of significant leadership. Part of the work of ending poverty is reversing this pattern, starting in our own social change efforts. So it is of utmost importance that an ally respects the leadership of groups and individuals who have experienced long-term poverty, and supports their self-determination and self-efficacy. An ally who is economically privileged should as much as possible try not to exert power over the decision making of people from less privileged backgrounds.

The meaningful leadership of our allies who are surviving poverty is a largely untapped resource, but one with amazing potential. Who could better understand the true causes, impacts, and potential solutions to poverty than the people who have been most directly impacted by it? Who could have more moral authority to lead our collective efforts for social justice? Who deserves a chance to determine their destiny? Authentic allyship organizations or groups, ones that are truly rooted in the practice of solidarity, understand this and take concrete steps to support it. Shared leadership is a key distinction between poverty industry organizations that <u>serve</u> people living in poverty versus allyship organizations that <u>partner with</u> people living in poverty.

Further, not only is shared leadership more just, it is more effective in the long run. I truly believe that once we can create shared leadership on a broad scale, which means respecting and supporting the self-determination and decision making of people who've been ignored and discounted so frequently by the wider society, then we will finally be able to come up with more creative, more effective, and more equitable strategies to create a just economic system.

Clearly, the issue of equitable leadership is very important to creating successful cross-class efforts, but there are obstacles to making it happen. Some of these obstacles may go back as far as childhood experiences. Those of us who grew up in the middle or owning class were often socialized into leadership positions that our peers from poverty may not have been. I remember that I was encouraged to take leadership roles from a very young age. For instance, I was selected and trained as a peer mediator in elementary school. As a peer mediator, I spent my recess trying to break up disagreements between my classmates before they escalated into fights. Although I don't remember too many details of the experience, that role as a peer mediator probably set up lifelong skills in analyzing situations and reacting calmly in the face of conflict, and most importantly thinking of myself as an authority figure who can be trusted to instruct others. These are skills I use every day in my professional work.

Then I think about my elementary school friend Josh. My friendship with him was basically structured around me trying to teach him methods of emotional control and conflict resolution so he wouldn't get into fights as often. At 10 years old, Josh and I were both just kids who had plenty of innate potential to mature into leaders. But we had different class backgrounds that were already affecting our paths. Because of our teachers' (and my) unconscious biases and because of material differences in our families' circumstances which may have come from generations of institutional disadvantage, I was the one with the Peer Mediator sash across my chest and a clipboard of conflict resolution techniques, and he was the one fighting on the playground. Josh, rather than getting the message that he was an authority figure who could be trusted to instruct others, was given the message that he was a trouble maker.

These early experiences of privilege or oppression do tend to get reinforced and amplified into lifelong divergences. Josh went on to become a teen parent and serve time in juvenile detention for arson. I lost track of his story after that. By contrast, I was valedictorian of my class and elected to leadership positions in student groups in high school. Then, as I got older, I pursued my college education at an elite liberal arts college. College taught me that my peers and my professors would value what I had to say and take it seriously, and that I had the right, indeed the responsibility, to critique anything I was taught and judge its veracity based on my own reason and experience. Later on in my professional life, I was placed in the front of a classroom. Even when it was a classroom full of adults who may have had far more life experience than I did, it was assumed that I was the expert and authority.

This is not to say that I felt perfectly comfortable and confident in all of these leadership situations. Often far from it. But I suspect it's a lot easier for me to trust myself in a leadership role given this history of recognition and authority than for someone who's been given covert or even explicit messages her whole life that she is a problem, not someone to be taken seriously, unintelligent or inarticulate. As Julia's poem says, a "problem and case to be managed." One of "those people."[142] Many people in poverty have been silenced in this way, and conditioned to believe that the only way to become knowledgeable is to receive knowledge from an outside authority, not to trust one's own ability to think and creatively solve problems.[143] Of course, many individuals who have experienced poverty are able to overcome these messages and become very talented and articulate leaders. I admire those who do, and can only imagine the internal strength that must take when leadership is not simply bestowed by circumstance.

In addition to these social psychological factors affecting leadership across classes, there are also practical dimensions that can make it much easier for economically privileged people to become leaders. Middle and owning-class allies tend to have access to resources, by definition. These resources may be social (knowing a network of people who can be supportive in some way), institutional (having influence in institutions where decisions are made or resources are controlled), material (access to transportation, space, communication tools, funding, or other resources that facilitate work) or personal (security in basic needs like housing, food and safety that allows one to focus on other things). Middle and owning-class allies may also be more likely to have professional roles where they can get paid to do their allyship work, which helps support all the other resources listed above and creates the critical resource of focused time.

All of these factors can converge to make it a lot easier for middle-class and owning-class allies to assume leadership roles in cross-class alliances. However, just because it's easy doesn't make it right. Part of the reason that poverty exists is the economic, social and psychological oppression of the poor, oppression which tries to limit people's capacity to exercise leadership in their own lives or in the broader society. So part of ending that oppression means facilitating leadership of people from oppressed groups. Trying to end poverty with only the leadership of privileged allies creates a contradiction. In Paulo Freire's words:

> True commitment to the people, involving the transformation of the reality by which they are oppressed requires... [that] the leaders cannot treat the oppressed as mere activists to be denied the opportunity of reflection and allowed merely the illusion of acting, whereas in fact they would continue to be manipulated—and in this case by the presumed foes of manipulation... By imposing their word on others, they falsify that word and establish a contradiction between their methods and their objectives. [144]

True allies must be more than "presumed foes of manipulation;" we must be the actual foes of manipulation. We must encourage and enable the meaningful decision making and action of allies of all backgrounds.

Perhaps more than any other topic, I feel that participating in the Allyship Project taught me personally a lot about effective leadership and how to try to make room for the leadership of others, even when it isn't easy. I certainly haven't mastered it, but I'm constantly seeking to be more effective as a developmental leader whose priority is developing the capacity of all. [145]

To chair or not to chair: When to hold back your leadership

During the Allyship Project, I was the only member of the group who had not personally experienced generational poverty. Thus, I reflected deeply on what would be the most appropriate role for me within our work. The Allyship Project was born out of my personal vision, so it was inevitable that I would have some sort of a leadership role. However, a fundamental point of our work was challenging the notion that economic privilege should always equal power and control. We were trying to teach and live a different way of working in solidarity—where everyone's voice had equal weight, where power was shared, and where the wisdom of people who had grappled with poverty was respected and valued. We had assembled a group of amazing community leaders, activists, mothers and grandmothers, and all-around wise women, all of whom had immense capacity for leadership and were leaders in their communities.

Trying to be a good ally, aware of my own privilege but not letting it guide my behavior, felt like walking a very thin line. On the one hand, I did have input into the group's direction and conversation. I felt that it was important as the middle-class ally in the room to sometimes state and even push for my opinions. I felt I had that right as an equal member of the group, but more importantly I believed that I was pretty useless as an ally if I wasn't true to my own values and opinions; if I was just a doormat who followed whatever my allies said simply because they were people of color or people from low-wealth.

On the other hand, I was very intentionally trying to check myself. A metaphor I used at the time was another one from elementary school. I learned from a very young age that I would usually have the answer the teacher wanted when she asked a question to the class. I also learned that I would usually be the first to raise my hand. I figured out that if I raised my hand right away every time I knew the answer, I would end up giving the answer 90% of the time and few of my classmates would ever get the chance to speak. So I didn't rely on the teacher to make sure she was calling on everyone fairly. I started self-regulating and not raising my hand every single time. I would wait and allow the other students in my class a chance to answer. Did that hurt me? Not at all. I still answered enough so that my teacher knew that I was paying attention and participating. And I personally knew that I had gotten the right answer, so my self-esteem wasn't in any danger.

What's the parallel to allyship? By self-regulating, I tried to hold myself back and leave room for the contributions and perspectives of others in the room. I tried to not always be the first to raise my hand or the first to speak. I tried not to give all the right answers. Although that's where the Allyship Project differed from my elementary school classroom. Unlike state capitols or multiplication tables, the questions we were asking didn't have only one right answer. And by not always giving my "right" answer first, I was more likely to hear the "right" answers of the others in the room, which I'm sure, in the end, made for a much better overall outcome.

If I had let my class patterns go unchecked during the Allyship Project's conversations, I would have probably assumed that I already knew everything there was to know about the concept of allyship from all my book reading. I would have probably taken up way too much of the air in the room. I would have probably been inclined to structure our meetings very formally and manage them very strictly in a way that might have felt alienating to some members. I would have probably tried to shut down any sort of conflicts as "unprofessional" or "irrelevant." As a result, I would have probably missed a lot of important insights that my allies didn't share because they didn't feel their thoughts would be valued. I would have basically learned nothing new, and then I would have wasted loads of paper and made a really boring workshop with a long PowerPoint full of technical jargon and abstract theories and concepts. Not what I was going for!

So I tried to not do that. I tried to not speak first, and occasionally on a few issues that I knew next to nothing about from my life experience, I didn't speak at all. I tried to make decisions collectively and ask permission before I represented the group in a certain way or asserted authority. I tried to let go of some of my expectations about how meetings would run or how a project works. If someone said something that challenged my previous assumptions or was something I disagreed with, I tried to consider it very thoughtfully as coming from an authority, even if I still didn't end up totally agreeing.

What were some of the benefits of acting this way? Well, for me personally I think it was a really healthy experience to try to limit my own leadership and practice being a good equal partner or even follower. In order for the work of ending poverty to be led by the people who have been most marginalized in the current economic system, middle-class or owning-class leaders need to get out of the way once in a while.[146]   As Mia McKenzie, an African-American, queer activist and author, says:

> If you are a person with a lot of privilege (i.e. a white, straight, able-bodied, class-privileged, cisgender male or any combination of two or more of those) and... you can recognize that part of the reason your opinion, your voice, carries so much weight and importance is because you are a white man (or whatever combination is working for you), then pushing back against your privilege often looks like shutting your face.[147]

As hard as that might be at first, it's really pretty easy. It doesn't hurt. Just like in elementary school, I still know that I have the potential to be a leader even when I try to hold myself back and make room for others to come up with their answers. And I'll end up learning a lot more in the process.

Of course, I did not find the perfect balance. At one point, the Allyship Project was writing a proposal to present our work at a conference and the proposal required us to identify someone as the chairperson. Some members of the group felt that since I was the founder and since I handled all the logistical communications, I should be listed as the chair. Other members felt strongly that it was very important that we publicly demonstrate an alternative to typical structures by not listing me as the chair. I felt a little caught in the middle, a bit frustrated that we even had to deal with the semantics of it, since in practice we tried to do our work collectively.

In retrospect, it was more than semantics. I think now I would side more strongly than I did at the time with not listing myself as the chairperson. Perhaps as a contact person, or a co-chair, but certainly not the sole leader. Even if it wouldn't make much of a difference to our mode of operation as a group, it might have been a learning opportunity for the conference organizers and participants.

At the very least, though, our discussion about how to handle the chairpersonship was a learning opportunity for me. It helped me reflect more intentionally about my appropriate role. In the years since, as I've had leadership roles in other diverse coalitions, I have tried to apply the same techniques of staying out of the way. I've also tried to expand on that practice by learning how to even more actively encourage leadership of marginalized people. Sometimes this has meant tactfully encouraging other middle-class allies to shut up and stay out of the way. And sometimes this has meant proactively inviting participation and leadership from allies from poverty. I know I have a lot of room to grow in looking for those opportunities and capitalizing on them quickly and respectfully.

A Tradition that Has No Name: Developmental leadership

> *I can't help but believe that when you bring everybody in, that something really important will happen. There might be new knowledge, insights, and strategies. There might be new bonds that will give people more courage and strength for the resistance.*
>
> *-Jane Sapp*[148]

Making room for and inviting the participation of others are not the primary roles of those we typically think of as leaders. We tend to imagine leaders spending a lot more time talking and persuading others than listening to them. But there's an alternative model of leadership that functions very differently from the kind we usually see in political, business or civic settings. Mary Field Belenky, Lynn Bond and Jacqueline

Weinstock, in their book *A Tradition that Has No Name*, identify this as "developmental leadership."[149]

Belenky, Bond and Weinstock profiled a group of women who had created grassroots organizations in the developmental leadership tradition. Their organizations existed to support the needs of women in their local communities and were run in an extraordinarily participatory, non-hierarchical way. In fact, the authors named these organizations "public homeplaces" because the nurturing they provided to their members and the mutuality of collective effort seemed much more like a family "homeplace" than like a traditional service agency or political advocacy organization.[150]

Despite significant differences in their missions and constituencies, the founders and leaders of these public homeplaces all exercised developmental leadership in some common ways. One of the most defining characteristics was listening:

> The homeplace women are all highly articulate leaders—indeed, most are extraordinarily gifted storytellers and spokespersons. Even so, when the homeplace women talk about their own leadership styles they invariably emphasize listening at least as much as speaking. While only a few of the homeplace women like to think of themselves as spokespersons, all of them—without exception—see themselves as the kind of leader who draws out the voices of people so that they might speak for themselves.[151]

To facilitate such deep listening, the leaders used dialogue and open-ended questions to encourage reflection.[152] They were genuinely interested in the opinions and experiences of the women in the communities they served—whether that was mothers reflecting on child rearing, folk artists reflecting on their art forms, or disenfranchised citizens reflecting on the needs of their neighborhoods. Often, the developmental leaders very intentionally recorded and celebrated all that they heard from these community members, for instance by creating works of art or formalizing stories into written histories. In this way, by honoring the voices of the people they worked with, they helped people start to honor their own voices more.

The public homeplaces weren't just spaces for conversation, however. They all encouraged their membership to become more active in the public sphere, hence the "public" side of public homeplace. This engagement took on different forms depending on the context, but in all cases it was decided upon collaboratively, based on the conversations nurtured together.[153] So as community members identified local needs, they developed plans and strategies to address those needs. Sometimes they took on the tasks themselves, such as setting up child care spaces that were safe and developmentally sound. Other times, the needs required them to confront political power structures, such as getting the city to convert an abandoned hospital complex into affordable housing. In all of these instances, the leaders supported their members to feel confident in their own ability to exercise leadership in a public sphere, sometimes in the face of fierce opposition.

Although this kind of developmental leadership is rare, it should be noted that not all of the leaders felt like they were inventing something entirely new. Especially the African American leaders profiled in the book recognized a well-established, if informal, tradition of such leadership among African American women in particular. One woman shared that "when she was a child growing up in the segregated South, such women leaders were known by the title 'Sister ----.' 'If a woman was called Sister So-and-so,' she said, 'you knew she was the kind of leader who dealt with big issues, a leader who was always working to lift up the whole community.'"[154] This is a wonderful example of how there can be hidden traditions of strength and leadership, even within oppressed communities. Those of us seeking to be allies should always be watchful for such leaders and support their work.

Developmental leadership is a powerful concept. However, much like the idea of allyship itself, if it is not practiced authentically, it could end up morphing into something totally counter to its true intent. Belenky and her colleagues consistently use the metaphor of mothering when talking about developmental leadership,[155] in part to distinguish it from other forms of leadership based on more traditionally masculine metaphors like war. But to organize a leadership tradition around a metaphor of mothering runs the risk of paternalism, or in this case maternalism. Listen for instance, to the following quote from one of the developmental leaders profiled in the book:

> Sometimes you get the feeling that your very hope is all that is holding someone up. You just got to keep holding the hope. You can't let down. It's like with babies. You just have to keep holding that neck until they can hold their head up on their own. You got to keep holding it no matter how much the baby is squirming and spitting. If you stand there and just keep holding the hope, eventually they too will believe.[156]

Now, this is a beautiful sentiment and a tender metaphor, and I have no doubt that the woman who said it is a true ally who lives out a deep and collaborative respect toward people from all walks of life. Even so, for me as someone attempting to be a novice ally rather than one with decades of community building experience, it would make me a little nervous to start referring to my allies as babies who can't hold their heads up on their own. It is true that we all have our vulnerabilities and certainly need the support of our allies from time to time. But people in poverty have been characterized for so many years, unconsciously or quite consciously, as immature or underdeveloped that it seems dangerous to proceed too far toward thinking of myself as a mother toward my allies. My allies are far more capable than helpless infants. The founders of the homeplaces, themselves, are fine examples of mature and competent leadership. Some of them grew up in communities marginalized by race or class, and even if not, as women they all faced sexism and prejudices about their capacity for leadership. By building and growing effective organizations, they proved themselves to be fully capable of holding their own heads high.

Even so, it can be easy to fall into the trap of "maternalism." We already discussed in Step Three how tempting it can be to over-diagnose internalized oppression or privilege in others. And especially if we fixate on the internalized oppression of our allies, it's a short hop over to maternalistically assuming that we have to "developmentally lead" our allies out of their internalized oppression. When someone else is broken or incomplete, we want to fix them. I certainly know that a weakness of mine is that I can sometimes be more apt to analyze someone's shortcomings than to search for their strengths. Focusing on someone's deficits or frailties rather than their capacities sets me up to be more of a fixer than a collaborator. I try to check that bad habit in myself, because I believe that it is absurdly presumptuous of me to either assume that my allies always need my fixing, or to suppose that I would even be capable of offering it, given that I haven't experienced that same form of oppression myself. Besides, I have my own internalizations to work on and overcome from my own intersecting oppressed/oppressor identities.

As it turns out, helping people heal from their internalized oppressions is a huge part of what developmental leaders in public homeplaces actually do, just with much more of an ethic of solidarity. True developmental leaders help people grow by focusing on building up their capacity, not fixing their imposed limitations. "As midwife leaders sponsoring the development of the excluded and the silenced, the homeplace women search for the strengths rather than the flaws of individuals and communities; they affirm what they see. They look for the 'growing edge,' trying to see people at their very best, trying to see where they are hoping to go."[157] By stretching their capabilities at their growing edge, individuals mature past their internalized oppressions, but not because any "fixer" has repaired them, rather because they have reconnected with their own suppressed potential.

Developmental leaders also practice humility by constantly reexamining themselves. They reflect carefully on what has gone well in their community work and what might have gone better. Even when they are disappointed by their allies, they refrain from blaming or scapegoating. "When goals are not met or if someone's performance is less than hoped for, the homeplace women simply ask, 'Why didn't this work?' 'What went wrong?' 'How could we have supported you to do a better job?'"[158] Implicit in asking themselves these kinds of questions, I would expect that the developmental leaders consistently examine their own internalized privilege and/or oppression (although Belenky and her colleagues don't use those terms) to make sure they aren't distorting their relationships and collaborations with others.

Finally, developmental leaders always recognize that, even as they are helping others extend their growing edges, they themselves are constantly learning from their allies, as much or more so than they are teaching. This keeps the leaders constantly find their own growing edge, and defining and pursuing new goals in relationship with others. Once again, listening is primary. The following inspiring summons to allyship comes from the same woman who spoke earlier about holding babies:

> I'm always afraid that I am going to miss a treasure that got thrown away because somebody didn't value them, because someone didn't like the color of their skin or thought they were too fat or too skinny. I am afraid that I'm going to miss some new answer to some important problem that got thrown away because no one took the

time to listen. I'd rather bring everybody in, rather than to have missed something really wonderful. I can't help but believe that when you bring everybody in, that something really important will happen. There might be new knowledge, insights, and strategies. There might be new bonds that will give people more courage and strength for the resistance. [159]

To the extent that those of us in allyship relationships seek leadership, we should be seeking to model ourselves after these amazing developmental leaders. For allies from economic privilege, who may have a long history of being encultured into less egalitarian styles of leadership, we should focus on the humility and restraint of developmental leaders, who don't grandstand and who ask the right questions to be able listen deeply to silenced voices. And for allies from poverty, who may have a long history of being encultured into believing they can only be followers, we should focus on the strength and fierceness of these midwife leaders, carrying on a tradition that has no name but a tradition of community leadership and influence nonetheless.

Defining a purpose

Now that we have explored alternative models of what leadership may look like in partnerships of solidarity, I'd like to return once again to the Allyship Project's definition of an ally, this time focusing on the first and last few words of it:

An ally is a person <u>who seeks to end poverty</u>, and who partners with people from all class backgrounds to work toward that goal.

An ally develops personal, responsible, respectful and mutually beneficial relationships with people from different class backgrounds than him/herself. These relationships are not necessarily friendships, but are at

> *least respectful working relationships bound together by*
> <u>*a common goal of ending poverty*</u>.

Allyship is goal-driven. As much as it is about relating to one another in a personal, responsible, respectful and mutually beneficial way, allyship relationships do not exist merely for relationship's sake. They exist for a common purpose of ending poverty and promoting a more just and equal economic system in which we can all participate.

This leads to a couple key points in regard to leadership. The first may already be obvious from what's been said, but deserves to be stated anyway. Allies living in poverty need to be a part of the work of ending it from the <u>very</u> beginning, when goals are first set. If allies from poverty are simply invited to support a pre-existing agenda, then they are probably being used, again in Freire's words: "allowed merely the illusion of acting"[160]. They have been "denied the opportunity of reflection" by not getting to help set the goals.

This can happen all too easily. Many organizations and initiatives have a core group of power players that set the agenda and strategy. Often the official "decision making" body, whether it be a board or other group, is in reality merely responsible for reviewing and endorsing the strategy devised by the power players. So if the core agenda-setting group is not inclusive of people from all class backgrounds, then even a stamp of approval from a more diverse board doesn't truly reflect an inclusive allyship effort. People living in poverty need to be included in defining the "common goal of ending poverty" to make it truly common.

A great example comes from Vu Le, the Executive Director of a nonprofit that works on leadership and capacity building in communities of color. Le tells a story about getting asked (for the thousandth time) to organize a focus group of people of color to advise an already operating (and well-funded) educational reform effort.[161] Le declined, since his organization was at capacity with their own projects. Then he used the opportunity to educate the representative of the other organization about how traditional "engagement" efforts are ineffective:

> Community engagement must begin at square one. Too often efforts get to square three or four, usually well-supported by funding at each step of the way, before people stop to realize, 'Hold on, we're not doing a good job reaching underrepresented communities.' They scramble and backtrack, but it may be too late, since funding usually has been allocated without these communities in mind. So then we get asked to participate without being provided resources.[162]

This is a classic example of a missed opportunity for true solidarity between communities that had common goals. Unfortunately, the organization with resources simply wanted to use the input of low-income people of color to support their pre-existing goals, not to share leadership and resources in a more meaningful way.

This is not to say that allies of privilege can't develop their own vision of social change. I had the vision of the Allyship Project. But I tried not to be rigid in imposing my ideas about how that vision would be carried out once I was actually working on it in solidarity with my allies. And, indeed, it changed dramatically! My initial plan was to conduct individual interviews. Instead, the project evolved into a collaborative group effort, supplemented by a few additional interviews. I know my own learning was greatly enhanced as a result of the shift in approach. I had a vision, but I worked with others to craft the actionable goals that guided our work.

Another point is that setting and working toward tangible goals is an important way to facilitate and deepen allyship relationships. A good example comes from the Highlander School in Tennessee. Highlander was an exceptional educational space where, beginning in the 1930s, many influential labor and civil rights leaders were trained.

Highlander taught what I would describe as the essence of allyship, and they achieved racial integration at a time when that was virtually unheard of in the South. One of Highlander's founders, Myles Horton, reflects on how they did it:

> We decided to hold integrated workshops and say nothing about it. ... People didn't quite understand how it was happening. They just suddenly realized they were eating together and sleeping in the same rooms, and since they were used to doing what they were *supposed* to do in society, the status quo, they didn't know how to react negatively to *our* status quo. We had another status quo at Highlander, so as long as we didn't talk about it, it was very very little problem. Then later on, participants started talking about it from another point of view, a point of view of experience. They had *experienced* something new, so they had something positive to build on. (emphasis in original)[163]

In the case of the Highlander School, the leaders carried out their principles of non-discrimination by simply living them, without any discussion or debate. Mind you, it should be abundantly clear by now that I support reflecting on and discussing how to have effective allyship relationships, rather than simply "saying nothing about it." But I also admire the Highlander approach. It was an uncomplicated way to approach an immensely complicated social issue, and it worked. I think part of what made it work was that Highlander's workshop participants had a purpose for being there beyond simply experiencing integration. They were there to participate in a workshop about another topic entirely. They were there to learn and to discuss with one another. In the process, they built an experience of racial cooperation and solidarity which became the most meaningful way to learn about race relations.

Cross-class relationships, too, will rarely move beyond the level of small talk if there's not a broader purpose—a mutually defined goal. The process of refining that goal and working toward it will build a "point of view of experience" of cross-class cooperation. That experience will likely include many positive things that help build trust and occasionally conflicts that challenge that trust. This is where I believe that being explicit and candid about internalized oppression and privilege and other dynamics present in allyship relationships helps us navigate them more effectively. This kind of dialogue is very important to successful allyship partnerships, as long as we ensure that we get back to the action at hand without getting bogged down in endless analysis.

What, then, is the action at hand? I've been purposefully rather vague about what allies actually do together. Partly this is intentional, because as we just discussed, concrete goals and action plans should be decided collaboratively and based on community needs, rather than decreed by some book, even this one. But I will admit that part of the vagueness is also because there are sadly so few models of authentic allyship to follow. There are a lot of organizations designed by economically privileged people to serve the poor, but far fewer that have been built in solidarity <u>with</u> people in poverty to pursue common goals. Still, there are some, such as the public homeplaces surveyed in *A Tradition that Has No Name*, or the Highlander Center, or work done by educators like Julia Dinsmore, Donna Beegle or Paulo Freire. So, in the interest of being slightly less vague, here are some ideas of the types of work allies might undertake together, in no particular order:

- Cultural work/Arts – This can most broadly refer to any artistic endeavors with a social justice component—art designed to inspire and encourage people to think more deeply about social issues. Cultural work also refers to a specific practice profiled in *A Tradition that Has No Name* of maintaining and strengthening the cultural traditions of the African American community as a way of honoring and uplifting the artistic heritage of the African diaspora.[164]

- Political advocacy – Includes lobbying and political action at all levels of government, as well as voter engagement and education. This may also include participating in citizen oversight or input boards or similar groups.

- Community organizing – This can include educating and mobilizing groups of people for political or economic goals.

- Formal and non-formal education – Covers a broad array of educational settings, including traditional K-12 or college education, adult literacy or professional education, community education, or small social learning and discussion groups where people come together to learn about social issues and social change.

- Community service – Providing some sort of direct service to the community in a collaborative way, whether that be childcare, job training, housing development, medical care or other urgent needs.

- Religious practice – Many religious traditions for centuries have provided service and advocacy on behalf of oppressed peoples, so allies who share common beliefs can worship together. They can also participate in all the other activities listed above as a moral or religious practice.

This is certainly not meant to be an exhaustive list. Many groups move within and between all of these different categories regularly. Also, as allies begin to work in solidarity with one another and to include more traditionally excluded voices, they will likely come up with novel and innovative new ways to partner together. This is one of the most exciting possibilities of working together as allies to define a mutual purpose – no one really knows where it might go and what all it might accomplish. As long as everyone has a voice in the process, crafting a vision of a shared future will provide a solid foundation for allies to come together in solidarity.

Alone together: Respecting constituency groups

Allyship is all about working together. Nevertheless, sometimes it helps to take a little bit of a break from being so inclusive. Ironically, sometimes the best way to deepen our relationships with people who are different than we are is to spend some time with people with whom we have more in common. Why is that, you say? Sometimes we have to find support from others who will just "get it" as we sort through our thoughts and feelings with regard to allyship. Sometimes we want to share our stories with people who've lived almost the same story and who therefore don't require us to elaborate as many of the details. Sometimes we need to be able to ask honest questions or vent about frustrations with less worry of offending someone. Sometimes we must seek support from the people who have known us the best, who can help us to recognize our own strengths and to define what we can bring to our collaborative efforts.

Constituency groups can provide all these functions. Constituency groups are gatherings of people who come together around a shared identity, usually temporarily, but sometimes for long-term support. They provide sheltered time that can help restore us and give us valuable perspective for when we come back into our diverse allyship coalitions. Constituency groups are one important strategy to address the emotional needs of everyone involved in pursuing solidarity. Dismantling biases and opening ourselves up to new ways of collaborating is stressful, even as it is liberating and enlightening. Designating time, resource people, and a peer group that "gets it" to help each of us process our learning is important.

Initiating these kinds of constituency groups can feel awkward, however, especially for people from privilege. It's easy to feel a little left out when our privilege usually grants us access to any conversation of which we'd like to be a part. Take, for instance, the following example from Jamie Utt, a white diversity and inclusion educator and consultant. He tells this story of a white "ally" failing to give people of color uninterrupted time:

> One of the things that I love about the White Privilege Conference is its commitment to accountable racial caucusing spaces where White folks can meet with other White people, holding them accountable as they process their feelings or learning and where People of Color can process without the intrusiveness of White privilege and oppression. In my experience, the White caucus can get pretty emotional, but the facilitators are trained and ready to hold people accountable to their privilege and process. I've also heard that the various People of Color caucuses can be pretty emotional, charged with anger and sadness and hope and community. The space is vital.
>
> Virtually every year, though, there is a White person who doesn't get the need for these spaces. A few years back, a White woman burst into one of the People of Color caucuses throwing herself on the floor, crying, asking for forgiveness, bemoaning her Whiteness and her role in oppression. And I honestly think this woman would have considered herself an 'ally.'[165]

There are many layers to this one example. Clearly, though, while seeking absolution for her privilege, this woman was actually imposing upon her "allies" in a very privileged way. The author goes on to state: "One of the more common and egregious mistakes supposed 'allies' can make is to expect emotional energy from those to whom we ally ourselves."[166] Sometimes, as allies the best way we can support one another's well-being and leadership is to stay in our own caucus, do our own processing, and not to expect our allies to always come to our emotional rescue.

This story also relates to respecting the cultural integrity of our allies, a dynamic we will explore in much more detail in the next chapter. In the interim, it will suffice to say that sometimes there are things we just have to do for ourselves, by ourselves. For instance, in Step Two we learned about Maria Yellow Horse Brave Heart's model of historical trauma.[167] Part of Brave Heart's approach to helping American Indian individuals and communities heal involves incorporating traditional cultural and religious practices into standard mental health practice. I would argue that American Indian healing ceremonies should be conducted within the culture by members of that culture. Even the most informed and sensitive ally would run the risk of cultural appropriation and disrespect if they attempted it, which are aggressions that have perpetrated trauma on American Indian nations for centuries.

Because class culture is more diffuse and has less of a sense of shared history, it may be harder to see when a "cultural" practice needs to be kept exclusive, and when it can be shared with allies. A good rule of thumb, though, may come from the practices of developmental leadership we observed earlier. If all parties are finding their growing edges and developing their leadership in solidarity, then a shared experience is probably mutually beneficial. But if anyone is getting to the point of trying to heavy-handedly "lead" someone else to growth, especially if it's a privileged person trying to "fix" a person with less privilege, then it's probably time for a little break to do some processing in our constituency groups before we return to our productive allyship relationships.

Supporting a new status quo

Myles Horton at the Highlander School teaches us that the easiest way to challenge the status quo is to simply set a new one. If we can successfully make room for all voices, look for and stretch one another's growing edges, collaboratively define our common goals, and allow ourselves some personal and cultural processing space once in a while, we would certainly have set a new status quo of developmental and inclusive leadership. But we wouldn't be finished. We also must be prepared to support one another in our new status quo of cross-class solidarity.

As we saw in Step Four with reference to developing poverty competent organizations, developing truly inclusive allyship initiatives will also require a significant investment of time and resources. People grappling with poverty tend to be short on both time and resources, so enabling their meaningful participation and leadership in social change efforts requires that we address those needs. We must be thoughtful of the material, emotional and spiritual support necessary to enable true solidarity.

As the Allyship Project stated in the definition of this step: *due to social and economic oppression, people in poverty are rarely given positions of significant leadership. Part of the work of ending poverty is reversing this pattern, starting in our own social change efforts.* But reversing patterns can be hard. Those conditioned to lead must learn to be quiet. Those conditioned to follow must learn to speak up. Those accustomed to having resources may need to learn to think about how someone could participate in social change efforts without the support of a paycheck, a running vehicle, child care, or health insurance. Those of us without formal leadership experience may need to learn a whole new vocabulary of budgets and strategic plans and outcomes tracking. We may all find a few a growing edges that are a little sharp and thorny.

But it's worth it. Supporting the leadership and listening to the voices of our unheeded sages like Julia Dinsmore can open up entire new dimensions for our efforts for justice. As she writes:

> I hope my storytelling will inspire other poor people to claim and use their own voices, because they are needed and valuable. I would so enjoy their company. Coming out of the class closet, in person and out loud, has been

a lonely wilderness experience. If that which conspires to silence poor people had hands, shame would be its thumbs. Shame gave strength to chokeholds that have stilled the sound of many precious wisdoms, and shame detours humanity's progress toward liberating ourselves from deadly consequences of selfishness. The brilliance, poetry, singing, lamentations, prayers and praises in voices of the poor go far beyond victim-speak. It is my hunch that our unspoken conversations are blessings deferred and that they provide the missing pieces of a road map that takes us to a home worthy of our hearts![168]

Step 6: Respect the Inherent Human Dignity and Cultural Values and Practices of Everyone

An ally recognizes that no one should be required to fundamentally deny or change their culture in order to achieve economic opportunity. An ally who is economically privileged must be careful not to assume that all people living in poverty want to "be like them" or "look like them." She should not impose her cultural values or practices during the struggle for economic rights and opportunity.

My senior year of college, I brought Julia Dinsmore to Macalester to present to my senior seminar in the morning and to give a public talk about poverty and her life story in the afternoon. To round out the day, I invited her and some of my classmates over for dinner after the presentation. I was very excited about the possibility of continuing our conversations in a more intimate setting at my apartment, so I planned what I hoped would be a welcoming and cozy little dinner party. I had warned Julia that I was a vegetarian, so it would be a meatless meal that evening.

I'll never forget Julia announcing during her presentation that dinner at Annaka's place was to follow, and anyone who wanted could join us for some "P.C. food." I gulped. First of all, I hadn't made enough "P.C. food" for the entire audience there in the chapel that afternoon. But more significantly, I was mildly offended that she seemed to be implying that my vegetarian meal would be unfamiliar and unappetizing. As it happens, having grown up as the only vegetarian in a family of meat eaters, I had learned to deliberately try to be a good ambassador for vegetarianism by not preparing politically correct food, or weird food, or whatever other aspersions my suspicious meat-eater relatives might throw at it. I knew that my uncles would never willingly eat tofu or kale or vegan "cheese," so I didn't serve those things in mixed company. For this particular evening after Julia's talk, I had prepared a bean chili (with regular old dairy cheese and sour cream as toppings for those who wanted them), cornbread and fruit salad. Nothing too weird. As it turned out, Julia and our other guests enjoyed the meal quite a bit. We had a great evening of conversation, a little bit of poetry and music, and plenty of tasty P.C. food to go around.

Julia has since made good friends with my cooking. She even gave a shout-out in her book to me and my roommate for sharing yummy vegetarian food.[169] Obviously, this particular little culture clash lasted just a moment and was pretty insignificant. But cultural misunderstandings between people of different backgrounds are quite common and sometimes have more serious consequences than just a little gentle ribbing. The truth is that our cultures, be they ethnic, religious, or class cultures, often manifest themselves in our choices of food, clothing, music, speech patterns, family dynamics, and many other deeply personal aspects of our daily lives. As our society has gotten increasingly diverse, we've gotten a little bit better at multiculturalism—accepting and embracing the diversity of cultures that make up our society, allowing people to express their cultural practices, and recognizing that our society is richer for its diversity rather than threatened by it.[170] We're certainly a long way from perfect at it. But just a short jaunt down the street in nearly any major city in the United States will reveal multiple languages being spoken, restaurants serving cuisine from all over the globe, and a colorful mosaic of fashions and styles.

Whatever progress we have made in accepting one another's ethnic and religious cultural differences, we tend to get a lot more hung up on class differences. Class culture is controversial. Many will argue that it doesn't even exist.[171] This is in part because the concept of a "culture of poverty" has historically been used to further stigmatize and dehumanize people living in poverty.[172] Some worry that acknowledging a <u>different</u> class culture can be a slippery slope to conceding to a <u>deviant</u> class culture, one characterized by unhealthy family relationships, lack of work ethic, and self-indulgence.

Conversely, I believe that acknowledging that class differences may exist is precisely what we need to do <u>to avoid</u> these ugly stereotypes. If we deny any differences and don't leave any room for them, then the only culture we'll acknowledge is that of the "default" middle-class culture. Anyone who steps outside it then becomes deviant or deficient. Sometimes, we may not even realize we're judging class culture when we mock or insult certain things, but we're judging it nonetheless. As Betsy Leondar-Wright points out:

> Few middle-class people would say we have prejudices against working-class or low-income people, of course. Our classism is often disguised in the form of disdain for Southerners or Midwesterners, religious people, patriotic people, employees of big corporations, fat or non-athletic people, straight people with conventional gender presentation (feminine women wearing makeup, tough burly guys), country music fans, or gun users. This disdain shows in our speech.[173]

When we deny class cultural differences, those of us with economic privilege will easily fall into a sense of uncontested cultural superiority. We assume that because our ways of behaving are correlated with higher incomes, they must be better. So we try to change poor people into middle-class people, not just materially, but culturally.

Many social programs intended to assist people in generational poverty are actually designed to teach them the social patterns of the middle class. Think of all the financial planning classes, parenting classes, language classes, and on and on. I remember being a part of an organization once that was lamenting how few people in poverty were coming to their free yoga classes. They thought the reason for this was that people in poverty were so socially excluded that they no longer had the self-esteem to feel they deserved yoga. It didn't occur to them that yoga tends to appeal to a fairly particular demographic (outside of its traditional practice in Eastern societies and religions) and carries certain cultural connotations, so maybe the folks living in poverty just weren't interested in a middle-class pastime. Or maybe they had more important things to do to keep their families fed, clothed and sheltered.

I will not deny that my work, too, has involved quite a bit of cultural instruction, which I will explore in more depth shortly. But even as I have taught my students strategies for surviving in an economic system that is generally mono-economic and culturally middle-class, I have tried not to let my instruction fall into the trap of cultural conversion. I want to teach my students to move within and between different class cultures comfortably, not to feel like they have to choose between them or abandon their own "inferior" cultural identity. I'm not trying to force my students to permanently become culturally middle-class as if it's the only acceptable way to exist. I don't want to teach, explicitly or implicitly, that middle-class cultural practices are inherently superior, just because they happen to be culturally predominant. Middle-class culture and middle-class incomes are correlated, but that doesn't mean one has to cause the other.

In this chapter I hope to explore the complicated interplay between accepting cultural differences while still teaching cultural flexibility, respecting cultural preferences while still being authentic to one's own culture, and building functional allyship coalitions without imposing dominant cultural practices. In the end, allies should seek to respect the human dignity of one another, whether that means we share the same P.C. food, or the same yoga poses, or not.

Learning from clients: "Professionalism" and code-switching

When I taught classes on job search skills to young adults receiving welfare benefits, few topics in class brought up stronger emotions than "professional" grooming and appearance. The subject provoked an animated and interesting discussion every time. Prior to that part of the interviewing lesson, we would cover handshake etiquette, posture and body language, how to dress to impress, all without much controversy. But then it would be time for other aspects of appearance. To introduce the topic, I would distribute to the class the "grooming standards" of a local employer, which included, in part, the following requirements:

- Tattoos must not be visible to guests. Bandages, cosmetics and hair are not considered acceptable for covering up tattoos.

- Extreme hairstyles, such as dreadlocks, are not permitted.

- No extreme hair colors. Highlights are acceptable only if they are considered to be a natural color.

- Fingernail polish, if used, should be close in value and complementary to the individual's skin tone. Polishes that are unacceptable include extremely dark, bright, neon, frosted or gold-or-silver-toned.

- Appliques, acrylic nails and nail sculpturing or decorating are not acceptable.

- Jewelry should be kept to a minimum. Only women may wear earrings. Earrings may be worn in the earlobe only. A maximum of two earrings per ear may be worn, provided they are matched sets. All other visible piercings, such as tongue piercing, are not permitted. [174]

Someone in class would invariably be incensed by one or more of these requirements. Tattoos, dreadlocks, applique nails or facial piercings would be defended with a passion worthy of the Supreme Court. Sometimes the advocate making the case wore such fashions themselves. As often as not, though, they didn't, but still felt that the grooming standards were unfair and quasi-discriminatory. To be perfectly honest, I agreed. I personally found these standards rather draconian. But as an instructor, they were enormously helpful. I had intentionally chosen something that would be provocative, and I usually amped it up even further by scrutinizing everyone in the class to see who would be ineligible for a job with this employer. "You've got purple hair; you're out." "You're out for fingernails." "Oops, I see that tattoo on your wrist." I was usually able to eliminate at least half the class.

I didn't do this to embarrass anyone. Quite the opposite. I used these provocative rules to build some solidarity between the students and to try to generate critical thinking about where these kinds of "standards" come from and how they are applied. I knew that my classes would be mostly made up of young people of color who had grown up in urban, high poverty environments. Their peer group had a very different sense of what was fashionable and "acceptable" than the (presumably) middle-class H.R. professional who had written these grooming standards. By making the discrepancy painfully obvious, we could move the conversation away from being prescriptive and absolute (You must not paint your fingernails green because green fingernails are bad) to subjective and relative (Some people have a problem with green fingernails, so if you wear green nail polish, they may make certain assumptions about you). We could also talk about the broader social implications of "standards of professionalism," such as how a prohibition on dreadlocks, while ostensibly race-neutral, would likely have a much more significant impact on job seekers of color.

I didn't want to delude my students into thinking they could wear wild hairstyles, tongue piercings, or long acrylic nails and not be judged for it in the workplace. They and I both knew that wasn't going to be the reality of a mono-economic world of employment. But I didn't want them to think that I was judging them for their fashion choices, or more importantly that they should judge themselves. "Professionalism" is often taught as morality. You should conform to a certain style of dress, speech, behavior and relationship because it's the <u>right</u> way to behave. In reality, professionalism is just a style. It's a culturally determined set of behaviors that are really pretty arbitrary. The type of appearance considered "professional" changes and adapts and melds just like any other vogue. And just like any other form of fashion, it's used to determine who's in and who's out; who's on trend and who's hopelessly backward; who's cool and who's pathetic. Professional style is only "better" because the dominant culture has declared it to be, and enforces that through access to economic opportunity.

As we learned in Step Three, Paulo Freire uses the term "cultural invasion" to describe this phenomenon. Cultural invasion occurs when the dominant group imposes its cultural values on everyone else.[175] It is one technique by which the oppressor class retains its dominance. In the quote that follows, Freire uses the language of "invader/invaded" or "colonizer/colonized" instead of "oppressor/oppressed," but the meaning is the same:

> For cultural invasion to succeed, it is essential that those invaded become convinced of their intrinsic inferiority. Since everything has its opposite, if those who are invaded consider themselves inferior, they must necessarily recognize the superiority of the invaders. The values of the latter thereby become the pattern for the former. The more invasion is accentuated and those invaded are alienated from the spirit of their own culture and from themselves, the more the latter want to be like the invaders: to walk like them, dress like them, talk like them.[176]

Sounds a lot like a typical interviewing class, huh? How to walk, how to dress, how to talk...

I tried to discuss professionalism with my students without buying into its intrinsic superiority. I didn't want to "alienate them from the spirit of their own culture" because sometimes there were beautiful things about their culture. Take tattoos for instance. Most of my clients who had tattoos were memorializing or honoring a loved one. I saw lots of tattoos of baby footprints or names of deceased family members or symbols with deep personal meaning. And in my clients' turbulent lives where photos or other mementos could easily be lost to the next eviction, why not carry a permanent remembrance on your very skin?

Then again, other aspects of urban culture are clearly more silly or vain, and some are just materialistic fads to live up to some hip-hop mogul's idea of ghetto fabulous fashion. But even the frivolous fashions of a rapper aren't intrinsically any more frivolous than the fashions of a Wall Street executive.

It always bothered me when some of my coworkers had so bought in to the "culture of the invader" that they would teach professionalism in a way that was disparaging to students. I remember one employment counselor who had a mirror in his office with a sign above it that read "Would you hire yourself?" I'll admit the sign made me chuckle a bit, but it simultaneously made me wince. How would it feel to see yourself in that mirror when meeting the counselor for the very first time, as a young mother on welfare, nervous about whether your new counselor was going to respect you or make assumptions about you like so many others had in the past?

Still, that mirror may have been there with the best of intentions. In my experience, the professionals who preached conformity most stridently had usually experienced some (or multiple) forms of oppression themselves, due to their class, race, religion or other identity categories. They'd personally felt the pressure to acculturate. They'd had to work extremely hard to achieve any recognition or success in their careers. They'd had to prove that they fit in, so much so that they had often completely bought in to the more superficial trappings of professionalism. They believed in the symbols of dress and "grooming standards," because those symbols signified that they legitimately belonged in the professional world. Or at least that's what they communicated to their clients, who were marginalized from professional success both superficially and substantively.

That is why we taught professionalism after all. Whether we approached it with the zeal of the converted or the skepticism of the cultural critic, we all knew our clients needed the skills to be able to pass in a mono-economic world. As I said earlier, to whatever extent our society has gotten marginally better at being multi-cultural with respect to religion and ethnicity, we've still got much farther to go with respect to class. We pass all kinds of judgments on people based on markers of class and for the most part it is still culturally acceptable to do so. Think of all the reality TV shows that portray poor people as comedic buffoons.[177] These attitudes carry over into real reality, too. It is commonplace to assume that because people don't speak with "proper" grammar, they must lack intelligence. It is commonplace to associate certain mannerisms or appearances with criminality and laziness (think hoodies or baggy pants). It is commonplace to attribute circumstances to irresponsibility or incompetence (think driving an unreliable or uninsured vehicle). Thus, given these cruel stereotypes, those of us trying to help our clients escape generational poverty teach them to guard what information they share, to present their appearance in a particular way, and to watch their diction. The need for acculturation is a reality, but it represents a failure of multiculturalism, not a failure of a "culture of poverty."

By teaching our clients professionalism, we are teaching "code-switching." Code-switching is a linguistic term for when speakers switch between languages or between dialects or modes of the same language. But it can also be used to describe cultural shifts that we all make as we move between different areas of our lives.[178] We all code-switch. For example, even those of us who are most steeped in middle or owning-class culture still adapt our behaviors slightly to fit the workplace. I speak to my family members differently than I speak to my coworkers. I dress differently on the weekends than I do during the work week. But for some people, the switches are more drastic and take more conscious effort. And practice. Once, a student of mine, reflecting on professionalism, said that he wanted to learn the language of the workplace so he could "put it on and take it off again like a pair of shoes." I couldn't have said it more brilliantly myself. He recognized the need to code switch, but still wanted to be able to put on his more familiar and comfortable street shoes at the end of the day.

Oral versus print communication styles

Donna Beegle's work also features a form of code-switching, a form, in fact, more closely related to the linguistic origins of the term. Beegle's primary academic field is communication studies, and she draws upon the work of the well-regarded communications pioneer Dr. Walter Ong.[179] Ong identified two predominant communication styles: orality (or oral culture) and literacy (or print culture). Oral culture is our natural way of learning and communicating as human beings. It emphasizes relationships and sensory information. Print culture is a learned way of communicating that has come about since the widespread adoption of printed media. It emphasizes analytical processing and linear organizing of information.[180] Ong stresses that both oral and print culture are valuable approaches and complementary skills, although people tend to emphasize their primary style and look down on the other as unsophisticated or wonkish, respectively.

Different global cultures have adopted print culture to varying degrees. But even within a societal culture, class can make a large difference in the degree of orality versus literacy. People living in poverty tend to use an oral-culture communication style, while middle-class and owning-class people tend to be more oriented toward print culture. (I should be explicit here that "literacy" in this context does not simply refer to the ability to read. Most oral-culture people are able to read, but that is not their primary or preferred source of learning and communication.) Donna Beegle uses a simple self-assessment to gauge one's degree of orality versus literacy.[181] Imagine that you aren't feeling well. Your symptoms are mild but a little different than any bug you've had before. What would you do first to find out more? Would you look up your symptoms online or in a medical reference book? Or would you ask friends and family to see if they've ever had a similar illness? Think about it for a second. What would you do?

The first approach is more print-culture; the second oral-culture. (And if you said consult a doctor or other medical professional, that counts as print-culture since doctors are presumed to be highly educated from print sources.) Print-culture people tend to most trust information from authoritative written sources, whereas oral-culture people tend to most trust information from close, loyal relationships.

Adopting a print-culture way of communicating has profound impacts on much more than just the reference sources we use to get medical information. Becoming accustomed to learning from text attunes us to think linearly.[182] Letters must go in a particular order to make words, words form orderly sentences, and sentences are usually organized by sections and paragraphs into discrete segments that are assembled linearly from start to finish to make a whole argument or story. By contrast, when we communicate orally, stories tend to skip around and refer to events past or upcoming. We interrupt one another in conversations (at least oral-culture people do) and there's body language and non-verbal cues that add rich contextual meaning. Oral communication is much more free-form, spontaneous, multi-dimensional and relational than print communication.

These tendencies often spill over into how people manage their lives and their relationships. Oral-culture people, by being so attuned to human conversation and relationships, tend to be great at "reading" people (no pun intended) and understanding social and emotional cues. They have a holistic and creative perspective on the world, and are able to adapt as circumstances require. Conversely, print culture teaches people to break things into discrete units, to plan and organize time, and to focus on one thing at a time. After all, you can't read and do anything else at the same time. As a result, print-culture people tend to be able to separate the immediate object of attention from its context, analyze cause and effect, set priorities and goals, and respond to others in a measured way.[183]

As you can probably tell if you have made it this far into this book, I am strongly print-culture. That certainly has its advantages. School, with its textbooks and vocabulary words and writing assignments, came fairly easily to me. I am able to be analytical and purposeful as needed. Although I'm still a long way from mastering the art of managing my time, I rely on tools like calendars and schedules to accomplish tasks, and that usually works for me.

But my print-culture orientation has its limitations as well. I can be rather dry and serious when I communicate, and although I'm relatively sensitive to emotional cues around me, I keep my own emotions very close to the vest. Sometimes that has been a challenge in my interpersonal relationships. For instance, I had a roommate in college who was delightful, though pretty emotionally volatile. She got upset with me once because she said I was cold. She would tell me things that were personal and important to her and I would respond with "huh." She took my response as judgmental; I thought I was being considerate. I was trying to thoroughly process what she had told me and take my time to craft a thoughtful reply that would respect her emotions. But she didn't want a psychotherapist; she wanted a friend who could offer immediate empathy.

Even if I'm still fairly reserved in interpersonal relationships, I would like to think that I have gotten better over the years at developing my oral-culture skills, especially in the classroom. In fact, students have occasionally recognized me for this. I remember once I gave an example of some topic we were discussing when one young lady, out of the blue, started chuckling. When I asked what she found funny, she said, "You always do that. You say things one way, and then you come back and say the same thing some other way. You tell a story that dumbs it down for us." On the one hand, I was quite flattered. She was recognizing a technique I used very intentionally to serve the needs of my oral-culture students. I'd use stories, concrete examples, repetition and role plays to convey information in multiple ways. And I'd make the stories relatable and personal so class was more like having a conversation with friends than discussing abstract concepts divorced from any context.

On the other hand, I had to challenge her statement that I was "dumbing it down." Making a concept more personalized, concrete and contextual is not dumbing it down. If anything, it involves a higher level of mental engagement than just memorizing a factoid. And I would often direct my students to do it as well. I would ask them to differentiate between examples, or to imagine scenarios integrating the concepts we were learning, or to role play the skill being taught. Sometimes they would do all of the above in sequence to engage with the material in an increasingly involved way.

For instance, when I taught résumé writing, I would define the objectives of a résumé accomplishment statement abstractly, then have the students analyze examples of accomplishment statements to determine how well they met the goals of the résumé writer, then create examples as a group, and finally write their own résumé. They'd also get to role play a hiring committee reviewing résumés to discuss what appealed to them or turned them off. By this point, they understood résumé writing from an employer's and employee's perspective and had practiced and developed their own skills writing effective résumés. Now, from a print-culture standpoint, I could have been done at step one, when I handed them a list of the objectives of résumé writing. After all, I had conveyed the necessary information, on paper no less. But for my oral-culture learners in generational poverty, who had many distractions going on in their lives, learning was only going to happen through repetition and practice in relationship with their instructor and their classmates, where the abstract facts could start to take on greater meaning and relevance. Dumbed down it was not. I tried to explain as much to my student that day and hopefully helped her let go of her own internalized denigration of her learning style.

Outside of an educational environment, what does the theory of oral/print cultures mean for allies working together? Firstly, it is beneficial to recognize that these communication styles even exist. Differences in orality versus literacy often cause frustrations for groups trying to collaborate without anyone realizing the true source of the conflict. Oral-culture people are falling asleep in front of boring PowerPoint presentations at a conference, while print-culture people are searching frantically for the handouts so they can take notes. Print-culture people are ready to move forward with the meeting's timed agenda while oral-culture people are busy "wasting time" catching up with one another, telling jokes, and building relationships. Oral-culture people are expressing their emotions, possibly about events not directly connected to the group's immediate task, while print-culture people want to "stick to business" and dispassionately analyze the issues ad nauseam. Do any of these scenarios sound familiar?

These kinds of conflicts may have an orality/literacy discrepancy at the root but they're usually attributed to personality differences (or deficiencies). Print-culture people think oral-culture people can't concentrate; oral-culture people think print-culture people can't relate; everyone's frustrated. Recognizing oral and print cultures can bring us to new understandings about these conflicts and help us navigate compromises.

Donna Beegle describes how learning about oral culture was liberating for her. "I finally had a language to describe my strengths and frustrations as I was being challenged to acquire print-culture skills. I was heartened by Ong's affirmation of the value of both styles of communicating and learning. I began to better understand ways in which each brings rich opportunities for human growth and connection."[184] So that's the next challenge for allies—to loosen our grip on our attachment to our preferred style and start to practice some of the skills of the other. Print-culture people can learn to be a little less attached to agendas, and oral-culture people can try to structure their stories with more of a beginning, middle, and end. And everyone can learn to recognize when communication styles may be getting in the way of effective communication.

There is an important caveat, however. Given that print culture is the dominant mode of communicating in Western educational and economic systems, oral-culture people usually have quite a bit of experience code-switching to print culture, but print-culture people may rarely have been forced to adapt in the other direction. Therefore, when working cross-culturally, it is probably more important for allies with economic privilege to try to adapt to an oral cultural approach than the other way around. Within our allyship relationships and organizations, it would be nice to rectify a little bit of the imbalance toward print culture present in most every other institution of our society. I would imagine that the public homeplaces described in Step Five are very oral culture friendly. This is probably part of what makes them feel so home-like and helps their members develop a voice (note the metaphor). In creating our own public homeplaces in solidarity with our allies, we can use practices like porch sitting (See Step Four) to form relationships and to collaborate together in alternative, oral culturally competent ways.

That said, helping our allies from poverty learn the skills of print culture is one way we can help them navigate the dominant systems. Donna Beegle talks about how she learned to better navigate print culture on her way to earning a PhD, the pinnacle achievement of literacy:

> My mentor Dr. Bob Fulford told me I was the most oral-culture person he had ever met. He said, 'I want you to gain the skills of print culture, because that is what you need to be successful in the workplace and in education. However, I want you to maintain your skills of oral culture, because many people in our society have lost the abilities to develop relationships, to see the big picture and to be spontaneous.' He felt that in order to take care of ourselves and our planet, people need to use the skills and strengths of each style in situationally appropriate ways. [185]

Fulford was clearly an excellent ally who understood the dynamics of poverty but still had a deep respect for the inherent human dignity and cultural strengths of people who had survived it.

Scaling the ivory tower: Privilege, access to education, and translating

There is another context in which allies from middle and owning-class backgrounds have choices to make about how to communicate—among other people with economic privilege. As we discussed in Step Three, cross-class alliances will likely include disparities in education. Consequently, allies from economic privilege may often find that their education grants them access to social circles of other economically privileged people and access to institutions and positions of power (in government, business, education, etc.) where decisions are made that may greatly affect the lives of families living in poverty. Generally the only people invited to these conversations and deliberations are highly educated, privileged people, most of whom have never experienced poverty themselves.

Sometimes this exclusivity can border on the ridiculous— Julia Dinsmore used to stage conference sit-ins because she was so tired of academics and professionals holding elaborate events to discuss poverty without including voices from those who'd actually experienced it.[186] She'd show up uninvited and disrupt the agenda to share her perspective, whether it was appreciated or not. However, it is rare to find an ally like Julia, who has first-hand experience with poverty and who has the courage to force her way into ivory tower discussions.

Even among those invited into the ivory tower, people who actually have had personal experience with poverty may be reluctant to speak up. The uncommon few who truly have lived a rags-to-riches story of growing up poor but pursuing higher education and a middle-class lifestyle may be nervous about "outing" themselves in predominantly middle-class environments, due to the shaming of our culture. So even when formerly poor people do end up at the decision-making table, they may not chose to be bridge allies in that context. Thus, most of the time, allies from privilege are likely to end up in a lot of class-segregated situations, where the echo chamber can get noisy.

There are a number of productive approaches to the issue of class exclusion in institutional contexts. One of the most influential, but most complicated, is to help people in poverty access education so they can get direct entrée to decision making circles. Donna Beegle cites education as the most important avenue out of poverty, and she tells how vital mentors were to her success in earning a GED, college degree, and finally a doctorate as an adult.[187] The support of her allies like Dr. Fulford was key to helping her believe in her capacity to be successful, a belief she hadn't had as a young single mother without a high school diploma. Beegle's research and teaching goes into much more detail than we can cover here about how to be an effective mentor to people in poverty pursuing education, but it's a great read for allies interested in pursuing that path.[188] Of course, higher education is time consuming and expensive, so it is not always practical or desirable as an immediate solution.

The other direction allies from privilege can go is to use their access to open up opportunities for people in poverty to communicate. This was the approach we tried to take with the Allyship Project. All our members contributed to developing and delivering our trainings. It was truly a group effort. Everyone shared their personal perspectives and talents, regardless of their class background or education level. However, when it was helpful, for instance in writing proposals for grant support, I used my education and my print-culture skills to communicate our work in a "professional" way. I still collaborated with the group to ensure that the core meaning of my writing accurately reflected the group's intent. My privilege helped my allies access platforms for communication that they may not have had otherwise.

This is an important strategy to maintain the dignity of our allies. It shows respect to make room for individuals to speak in their own voice, rather than have someone else speak for them. Also, challenging the class/education elitism is a way to challenge the privileged assumption that more education is equal to greater intelligence. Don't get me wrong: I'm a fan of education and I think it is a resource that should be much more equitably shared. But I also know lots of brilliant people without letters behind their names. A couple of Julia's other favorite sayings are that she has a "Ph-Do," and that after her experience budgeting a meagre welfare check to shelter, clothe and feed a family, she could balance the state budget in an hour! What's so hard about balancing a budget when it has millions to go around? Seriously, it is important to recognize the innate and experiential intelligence of oral-culture people from all class backgrounds and not presume that everyone wants an advanced degree.

Unfortunately, though, the world will not always recognize Julia's "Ph-Do" and accord it equal value. Thus, she has told stories of using "class translators" who can say the same things that people in poverty might say, but in a way that will be taken seriously by those in authority. While "translating" should never be necessary, in some situations it is a legitimate, if unfortunate, strategy. When privileged allies find opportunities to use their institutional access to translate and to break down stereotypes to avoid class-based misconceptions, they should do so. They should educate others from privilege and represent the interests and needs of those living in poverty.

Furthermore, the best translators will also find ways to open up doors whenever possible for the direct communication of people who have experienced oppression. Translators can challenge the oppression that is built into their role by encouraging people with privilege to be quiet for a moment and listen to others speak on their own terms.

P.C. food: Being authentic but accessible

Thus far, we have focused on two arenas in which class culture may impact behavior: in adapting to "professional" standards, and in communication styles. In both cases, there is a tension for allies between honoring the cultural practices that are usually belittled and dismissed by the broader society, and at the same time helping our allies from poverty gain access to that broader society, which may necessitate at least temporarily adopting more middle-class behaviors and patterns. Working together as allies to develop language about these class differences and our strategies for code-switching between them will help us affirm their equal value. We can be upfront about the choices in front of us without automatically reverting to the dominant "better" middle-class cultural patterns within our relationships and organizations. As I would tell my students, you can make any choices you want, including tattoos and purple hair. And although I can deal with tattoos and purple hair in my classroom, and employers should be able to deal with tattoos and purple hair in the workplace, not all will. So as long as your choices are informed, go ahead and make them.

Allies with economic privilege have choices to make as well. As I already stated, there is much value to be gained in expanding our competency and tolerance for other cultural practices. Learning, or, really, re-learning the skills of oral culture can help us be more spontaneous and attuned to others around us. Letting go of some of our more rigid and arbitrary assumptions about appropriate behavior help us appreciate the beauties of other lifestyles.

At the same time, there are some potential pitfalls for allies from economic privilege. One danger is being completely inauthentic in an effort to relate to others. Inauthentically trying to co-opt another person's culture is not respectful; it's just obnoxious. In my case, as much as I didn't want my students to think that they were unintelligent just because they didn't always use "proper" formal English, I didn't start adopting their slang to try to earn their respect. I might have given them a laugh, but I wouldn't have earned much respect.

There's a balance to be found here. On the one hand, I tried to exercise my cultural competency enough to give my students cues that they could feel comfortable being themselves. I would code-switch a little bit to be less formal and more oral-culture. It would usually take some time of testing one another out until we found our boundaries and the students realized they were in a safe space. But I didn't try to speed up that process by pretending to be someone I was not. Rather than a code-switch, I suppose it was actually a code-shift. Just a subtle shift in my own behavior, as well as being very intentional about my reactions to others' behaviors to not even mistakenly give the impression of being judgmental.

I'm sure I never found the perfect code-shifting balance between staying true to my identity but open to others'. I must have done alright sometimes, though. I distinctly remember one occasion when a new student was a little nervous about speaking candidly with me. A friend of hers who had known me for a while (and who was very oral-culture and urban) said, "Nah, she's cool." That felt like a great compliment about my ability to bridge communication gaps, at least with that one person.

It may not seem fair that people living in poverty are asked to mimic the dominant middle-class culture in education and in the workplace, while middle and owning-class people are warned against being "inauthentic" and told not to stray too far from their cultural comfort zones. It isn't fair. It is clearly a double standard. However, there are important historical reasons for this particular double standard. When people from a dominant culture move into an oppressed community's cultural space without having been invited in, it is not only inauthentic, it can amount to cultural appropriation. This is especially problematic for many communities of color. African American music and other art forms have been appropriated for centuries. Religious traditions of Native American peoples have been usurped by all manner of spiritual seekers, even while Native American nations themselves were prohibited by law from exercising their spiritual practices.[189] There are many other examples. Therefore, as someone seeking to be an ally to oppressed communities, you will do best to carefully avoid code-switching your way into appropriating someone else's culture. On the other hand, if you are invited into an ally's cultural practice, feel honored and grateful. Even a simple, "Nah, she's cool," is a gift.

Finally, even as we remain authentic to our true selves, we can also practice our code-shifting to make sure our personal cultural practices aren't alienating or inhospitable to others. Up until now, we've talked about middle-class culture as if it's a monolith of buttoned-up, print-culture professionals. Of course, we know that's not true—all cultures include vast variations of expression and values. In particular, many middle and owning-class people involved in social change efforts may very intentionally adopt some counter-cultural practices and may feel very strongly about them. For instance, where I went to college among a predominantly liberal group of economically privileged young people, there were some very particular social norms. Most people dressed in a rather artistic style—usually some combination of thrift store hand-me-downs, fair trade natural fibers, and whatever else had gone through the laundry moderately recently. A lot of people embraced eco-conscious living by using alternative modes of transportation, minimizing their consumption of carbon-heavy foods like meat or imported produce, or recycling and composting at every opportunity. Openness about sexuality was encouraged; openness about religion made people a little awkward. There were a lot of political slogans and buttons; there were fewer haircuts or razors. It was a very particular subculture, and not one that everyone would embrace.

It is an admirable thing to live out one's principles through one's daily life. But if those practices go so far as to make others feel uncomfortable or judged, they may become a barrier to productive allyship relationships. For instance, John Anner shares the following anecdote about clothing: "The low-income women on welfare would turn out dressed as if they were going to the Sunday social, and all these middle-class activists from Harvard and Boston College would turn out in Salvation Army clothes, having invested very little in personal hygiene products. That's something that used to annoy me about middle-class folks, who dressed down because they didn't want anybody to think they were rich, while the poor folks dressed up because they wanted to be taken seriously."[190] Insisting on the righteousness of one's grungy hygiene standards or P.C. food over the opportunity to share a meal with someone and build a relationship seems excessive to me.

Consequently, those of us with intentionally chosen counter-cultural practices can look for opportunities to code-shift. For my part, I am unwilling to give up 20 years of vegetarianism. But I can make a meal with ingredients that will be familiar even to non-vegetarians, and try not to be heavy handed or didactic about my food choices. A code-shift. Or I can tell more stories, and repeat my examples in different ways to accommodate oral cultural learners in my classroom. Code-shift. Or I can collaborate with a poet to create a workshop on allyship, and leave the PowerPoint presentation at home. Code-shift.

Most importantly, I can let go of any assumption that my allies should walk like me, dress like me, or talk like me. *An ally recognizes that no one should be required to fundamentally deny or change their culture in order to achieve economic opportunity. She should not impose her cultural values or practices during the struggle for economic rights and opportunity.*

But, if anyone asks for my recipe for vegetarian bean chili and cornbread, I will happily share it.

Step 7: Recognize the Unique Contributions You Can Make to the Common Purpose of Ending Poverty

No human liberation movement in the history of humankind has ever progressed without allies. So the work of ending poverty will require the gifts and talents of everyone, no matter what class background they come from.

When I first started volunteering with A Minnesota Without Poverty in 2006, I quickly recognized that although the organization had mobilized an awesome group of dedicated social change makers, we were not a very diverse coalition socioeconomically. Julia Dinsmore was one of the few people involved in our movement to end poverty who had actually lived in it. She frequently pointed out that she would like some more company and she gently chided the middle-class leadership team about creating a more inclusive and diverse coalition. They, too, admitted the issue and earnestly wished it to change. A committee had even been formed to try to diversify the organization along class and cultural lines. But by the time I came on board, the committee had fizzled out and little action was actually being taken. I offered to take over chairing the committee.

I began by, at Julia's suggestion, re-naming the committee to "Let's Have Coffee." The mission of the Let's Have Coffee Committee was to host informal social get-togethers like coffee klatches, bowling outings, or potlucks (a venerated Minnesota tradition). We wanted to host casual events where people from different backgrounds could interact in a relaxed way and build trust with one another.

We planned a variety of fun events, we invited people we knew... and... no one came. I remember once dejectedly sitting in a bowling alley with my boyfriend and maybe one other member of our committee. What was I doing wrong? What was it going to take to get people to want to participate, to make time in their busy lives for the priority of building relationships with allies across class divides?

A few weeks later I figured out what it was going to take. The answer came at a retreat with many of the other volunteers involved in A Minnesota Without Poverty. During the retreat we took a Strengths Finder assessment.[191] I learned that my strengths were Intellection, Input, Learner, Connectedness, and Responsibility. If you're not familiar with the language of the Strengths Finder, this basically told me that I am a serious bookworm who likes to learn new things, ponders them deeply, and gathers copious amounts of information about any one subject. I also view the universe as interconnected and take the commitments I make very seriously. Although it seemed accurate, I have to admit that I was a little disappointed with my results. I hoped for something with a bit more people skill and a little less cerebrum.

But that was the point. My strengths were cerebral, not charismatic. Nothing in my list of strengths was about inspiring action in others, persuading those around me, or building relationships. I was not a W.O.O. (stands for Winning Others Over in the Strengths Finder lingo[192]). And the Let's Have Coffee Committee desperately needed some woo. I had identified the problem. It was me. What it was going to take for the committee to be successful was someone other than me to lead it.

That was one of the first times that I learned that just because one sincerely desires for something to happen and believes deeply in the need for it, doesn't necessarily mean that you are the right person to make it happen. Or at least not to make it happen in the way you might have initially expected. My strengths (both the ones I have and the ones I don't) taught me that I am not a community organizer. I admire those who can do that important work, but I am unlikely to ever be very effective at it. Nor am I an artist who can inspire others to action through creative mediums. I am not even the best administrator to keep the details organized. I do it when I have to, but I have never truly mastered the art of responding to emails in a timely way or keeping a tidy desk. But I can think. And I've developed a bit of a knack for teaching. And I listen carefully and deeply and find connections between things and people others may see as totally disparate.

Years later I came across another perspective that helped me come to more peace with my personal strengths and limitations. Paulo Freire, in his later years, sat down to have a conversation with Myles Horton, the founder of the legendary Highlander School in Tennessee.[193] Paulo and Myles were congruous souls in many ways, even though they came from different continents and spoke different languages. When they met to discuss their lives and work, they generously recorded some of their conversations so future generations could be flies on the wall to their insightful dialogue.

In those conversations, documented in the book *We Make the Road by Walking,* Freire and Horton reflected on the difference between organizing and education.[194] Both men believed that the two functions complement one another and should inform one another. But within movements for social change, they believed they may be carried out by different people at different times. Organizers focus on achieving particular outcomes, whereas educators focus on developing the people's understanding and problem solving capacities, even if the problem at hand doesn't get solved in the short term. In Horton's words: "If you were working with an organization and there's a choice between the goal of that organization, or the particular program they're working on, and educating people, developing people, helping them grow, helping them become able to analyze—if there's a choice, we'd sacrifice the goal of the organization for helping the people grow, because we think in the long run it's a bigger contribution."[195]

This was so comforting to me. Here were these two amazing leaders, whom I admired, validating the educators and the thinkers. Maybe it should have been obvious to me, but it wasn't. In many ways, utilizing my brain seemed antithetical to the kind of ally I sought to be. Without giving it fair consideration, I was picturing most intellectuals as locked away in their ivory towers, far removed from the realities of everyday struggles. It seemed like the community organizers were the ones with their feet on the ground, doing the gritty work of social change in solidarity with others.

The truth is, all of us have unique gifts to contribute to the process of creating a more just society. Even the bookworms like me. All our contributions are important. We can all find our own particular way to get our hands dirty, shoulder to shoulder with our allies.

As we discussed in Step Five, while bringing together the diverse talents of all our allies to work in solidarity, we need to make special efforts to include those who have been historically marginalized and support their leadership. However, that does not come at the expense of the gifts and capacities of anyone else. Whether it be by virtue of our innate strengths and talents, our personalities, or our experiences of privilege and/or oppression, none of us will approach obstacles in the same way or come up with exactly the same solutions.   Which is perfectly wonderful!   The joy (and challenge) of solidarity is to find ways to include all those strengths and approaches and experiences into a collaborative movement for progress. *The work of ending poverty will require the gifts and talents of everyone, no matter what class background they come from.* We need everyone to bring their best self.

In the following chapter, the final step toward becoming a better ally, we will explore how to discover and honor your unique capacities to contribute to social change. We will also delve into issues of motivation, which are especially complex for middle and owning-class allies. Honestly examining our motivations and making sure they don't come from unhealthy places, as we've already alluded to during conversations about guilt and shame (Step Two), paternalistic leadership (Step Five) or cultural invasion or appropriation (Step Six), is a critical part of showing up in solidarity in a genuine and respectful way. We all need to bring our gifts, and to bring them with integrity.

Models of social change

Linda Stout is a community organizer who grew up in poverty herself and has worked with very low-income communities in North Carolina and across the country. When Stout began her social justice career, she, like me, also had a bias toward community organizing as the only effective way to create social change.[196] Unlike me, she was actually quite gifted at it. But even so, with time she learned that other approaches are important as well. She and members of her organization now work from a four-part model for social change,[197] which includes:

- Organizing – "Organizing involves building relationships, providing training and education around issues, and mobilizing people to take action."

Figure 3. Theory of Change Circle.[196]

- Reform – "Reform involves changing laws and policies, or in many cases, trying to protect current policies that serve the public. Reform is often a compromise position, but it is critical to keeping situations from getting worse while we work on changing overall systems." Reform also includes human services work.

- Alternatives – "Creating models and ways that we can do things once we have changed the institutional systems, structures and laws that we believe cause the problems we are fighting."

- Consciousness shift – "Before people move to action—before the culture can change—their consciousness, or way of thinking first needs to change. Changing people's thinking happens through education, media, art and music, experience, feelings, and, sometimes, laws that require them to change the way they're used to doing things."

Linda Stout has come to believe that when people practicing all four methods of social change collaborate and share information and strategies, then they can build truly collective community power. I agree that all strategies are valuable. I also like how her model sidesteps a lot of potential argument and grandstanding over the value of one philosophy of social change versus another. All are useful and necessary and the strengths of one can often complement the weaknesses of another. Where Reformists compromise, the creators of Alternatives encourage us to think expansively and creatively. Where the Consciousness Shift dreamers and artists may lose touch with the real world, Organizers are rooted in it. Where the Alternatives might be too insular, Consciousness Shift brings the message to a wider audience. And where Organizers might alienate some with their bold demands, Reformists meet immediate needs.

Many of us will also work in ways that cross boundaries and blend categories. For instance, intellectuals and academics might be simultaneously working toward cultural shifts, designing alternatives, or negotiating reform. Service providers sometimes merge into community organizers. And so on. I appreciate that this model helps us to respect all the approaches people take to social change. It also encourages us to strategize about how our own work could cross more boundaries, or at least how we might collaborate more effectively with others trying different things. Where does your work and that of your allies fit into this model? How might you be able to build more collective power by working in solidarity with allies with different approaches?

Ally is an action: Finding true praxis

> *Human activity consists of action and reflection: it is praxis; it is the transformation of the world.*
>
> - *Paulo Freire*[198]

Another concept that can help us discover how we can make our best personal contributions to our allyship coalitions comes, again, from Paulo Freire. He describes "praxis" as a constantly intertwining balance between "action" and "reflection."[199] By action, Freire refers to political activities that one might undertake, whether that be organizing a labor union, teaching a class, leading a protest, producing a work of art, or running for political office, for example. Actions are designed to achieve some sort of particular outcome. And the best actions are undertaken in solidarity with and driven by the leadership of oppressed peoples.

Reflection, by contrast, is the more introspective half of praxis. Reflection involves developing *conscientização*,[200] or a critical consciousness, that is capable of comprehending and critiquing oppressive social structures. Reflection includes deeply personal examination of one's biases and assumptions, as well as social learning and dialogue where entire communities of people work together to achieve *conscientização*. Many of the topics we've explored leading up to this chapter fall into the category of reflection—educating oneself on the realities of poverty and economic inequality in our society, grappling with one's own internalized oppression and/or privilege, healing from historical traumas, resisting cultural invasion, understanding one's class-based learning and communication patterns, etc.

The defining feature of praxis is that it must include <u>both</u> action <u>and</u> reflection. Neither is adequate without the other. Without action, reflection turns into self-absorbed pedantry. Without reflection, action turns into aimless catharsis. Instead, Freire asserts that action and reflection, together as praxis, complement and reinforce one another.

> The insistence that the oppressed engage in reflection on their concrete situation is not a call to armchair revolution. On the contrary, reflection—true reflection—leads to action. On the other hand, when the situation calls for action, that action will constitute an authentic praxis only if its consequences become the

> object of critical reflection.... Otherwise, action is pure
> activism.[201]

As I recounted, in my own development, I had to learn to make greater peace with my reflective side. Reflection came more naturally to me, but, ironically, I valued it less. I prioritized action, perhaps because it was harder for me to achieve. By considering Freire's definition of praxis, I was able to come to a more balanced place, where I could see that my natural tendency toward reflection would be more meaningful if it took place in the context of active engagement with the world. Simultaneously, the actions that I took could become a part of my reflections, which in turn would prepare me to act in a more productive and inclusive way in the future. Finally, praxis taught me that I needed to pursue action (and reflection) not in isolation but in solidarity with others. Reflection can rather easily become a solo activity, but it is richer when it involves dialogue with others. Plus, as we've said before, ally is a relational word. The Allyship Project was one attempt to achieve shared praxis.

Another wonderful thing I learned about the concept of praxis is that it, too, affirms the value of a diversity of gifts among allies. Action is one half of praxis, but to be active doesn't mean that one has to be an "activist." As mentioned in Step Five with regard to setting goals for an allyship coalition, allies may work in solidarity together to provide services to their communities, to worship together, to educate others, to create art and sustain culture, OR to lead a protest. And all of these activities can further reflection as well. Praxis is a flexible concept that we can incorporate into many different contexts.

Privilege, print culture and praxis

One obstacle to praxis occurs when people assume that only some individuals are capable of reflection, leaving only action for others. As you might surmise, internalized privilege often leads people from middle or owning-class backgrounds to presume that they will naturally be the more reflective, even perhaps that they can do all the reflecting for everyone. Freire has no patience for this idea whatsoever. In fact, we have already seen some of his words on the topic in Step Five:

> True commitment to the people, involving the transformation of the reality by which they are oppressed requires... [that] the leaders cannot treat the oppressed as mere activists to be denied the opportunity of reflection and allowed merely the illusion of acting, whereas in fact they would continue to be manipulated—and in this case by the presumed foes of manipulation.[202]

We can see now that this statement is about praxis and how it must include everyone, most importantly oppressed people. "The revolutionary effort to transform these structures radically cannot designate its leaders as its *thinkers* and the oppressed as mere *doers*" (emphasis in original).[203]

This parallels our discussion about developmental leadership in Step Five. As we learned there from the founders of the public homeplaces, we cannot designate the leaders as "developers" and the oppressed as merely "to be developed." We've all got some developing to do, oppressed and oppressor alike. We've all been fed misinformation to make us accept the unjust system in which we live, where most of the economic benefits go to a very few elite capitalists. This makes it difficult for any of us to achieve anything close to *conscientização*. While it may be especially burdensome for people living in poverty who are subject to greater shaming and scapegoating, oppression, as Freire would say, damages <u>all</u> people's humanity.

Interestingly, Freire and the developmental leaders profiled in *A Tradition That Has No Name* use very similar methods to achieve critical consciousness and to develop people's powers of reflection (and action).[204] We've already seen that dialogue and posing questions are integral parts of developmental leadership. They are also fundamental to Freire's liberatory pedagogy. I will not go into Freire's methods in great detail here, but for anyone interested in education, whether formal or informal, I would highly suggest studying Freire's *Pedagogy of the Oppressed* if you're not already familiar.[205] For our purposes here, I will just reiterate one more time how important it is for people trying to be allies (especially those working to overcome their internalized privilege) to listen well, be open to learning from others, and let go of any need to have all the answers. Once again, Freire said it best:

> To achieve this praxis... it is necessary to trust in the oppressed and in their ability to reason. Whoever lacks this trust will fail to initiate (or will abandon) dialogue, reflection, and communication, and will fall into using slogans, communiques, monologues, and instructions... Political action on the side of the oppressed must be pedagogical action in the authentic sense of the word, and, therefore, action *with* the oppressed. (emphasis in original)[206]

A related challenge to praxis comes in communication patterns. We saw in the previous step how tendencies toward orality versus literacy can produce vast communication gaps. And for print-culture people, trying to talk about and develop a critical consciousness can get really print-y really fast. Much of the jargon in this very book—economic privilege, internalized oppression, the non-profit industrial complex, orality versus literacy, praxis—was defined and ellaborated in print-culture academic contexts by print-culture scholars who were used to communicating to print-culture audiences. Even Paulo Freire, who spent much of his career working with illiterate peasants (who must have been extremely oral-culture) still has a writing style that is notoriously dense, full of philosophical references and obscure vocabulary.[207] Consequently, I have seen a lot of print-culture people (perhaps myself included) get very lost in the weeds of academic prose when trying to talk about these issues. I've been to workshops about social justice that became little more than vocabulary lessons. It seemed to be assumed that defining social justice concepts is the same as grappling with them on a deep interpersonal level, or worse yet, equivalent to actually doing something about them.

How can print-culture people break out of our self-imposed complexity to dialogue about praxis in a more authentic way? First of all, in my opinion it is not necessary to let go of the jargon entirely. Developing accurate language is helpful. And we certainly shouldn't assume that oral-culture people are incapable of understanding complex concepts or achieving critical consciousness. Far from it. Their lived experience gives them a deep understanding of the true depths and mechanisms of oppression, once they can name it as such. Collaboratively developing a common vocabulary to name our experiences is an important way to overcome shame and isolation.

Nevertheless, as much as we can make use of the vocabulary, we should not get too enamored with it. We can also communicate very complex ideas using story, song, poetry, or other art forms. For instance, Freire's methods often included using pictures to stimulate dialogue and reflection.[208] The more we can incorporate oral-culture and artistic communication skills, the richer our conversations and storytelling will become. As I've told my students, stories don't dumb anything down. To the contrary, the layers of meaning in a good story help us engage with ideas on even deeper levels.

I saw this at work when our Allyship Project team led workshops. We had a beautiful mix of oral and print-culture styles in our group, and we used it to full advantage. Our workshops incorporated everything from spoken word poetry to reading analysis to spiritual centering practices to personal story to reflective dialogue to stand-up comedy. As a result, we connected with our workshop participants on multiple levels and created a more engaging and impactful workshop than if it had been one style alone. Similarly, I've tried to replicate that as best I can in my writing here, by telling many stories (using oral-culture skills) of my own experiences and those of my allies and mentors, to balance the more analytical and prescriptive (using print-culture skills) portions of the book.

Related to storytelling, Donna Beegle also talks about three levels of interpersonal disclosure and communication, building off of Kenneth Burke's identification theory.[209] The first level involves communicating only impersonal, factual information. The second level involves disclosing some details about one's thoughts or autobiography, but still in a rather distant way. At the third level, one shares things of genuine personal importance, including opinions and beliefs, personal history, and candid emotions. According to Beegle's research, oral-culture people are much more likely to be invested in learning with and from others if they have mutually achieved the third level of communication.

For example, she tells a story about herself as a young mother in her twenties who started participating in an intervention project focused on education. [210] Initially interested in little more than the housing subsidy she could potentially get by participating in the group, Donna Beegle found herself more and more invested as the facilitators of the group opened up about their own personal backgrounds. Even though all the facilitators had lived in middle-class circumstances, and therefore were not sharing stories that matched Donna's life experience, hearing their stories helped Donna feel that she could trust these women. Also, hearing about their privileged lives started to demystify economic success, and helped Donna realize that perhaps she and her family were struggling with something bigger than just their own ineptitude. This realization proved critical to her decision to take the risk to pursue her GED, as the facilitators of the program kept encouraging her to do. A decade later, Dr. Donna Beegle had multiple degrees and her life was on an entirely different trajectory.

By sharing our stories with one another, we can uncover new depths of reflection and praxis. Through dialogue, whether it's formal print-culture analysis or a good ol' oral-culture yarn, we can start to imagine new possibilities for our work together. We can start to see how our unique individual contributions fit into the bigger picture. However, this begs the question of <u>why</u> we fit into the bigger picture. What motivates us to seek social change in solidarity with others? Why bother?

Why have you come? Subjective need and common liberation

Our Allyship Project group was unequivocal in our belief that: *No human liberation movement in the history of humankind has ever progressed without allies. So the work of ending poverty will require the gifts and talents of everyone.* All class backgrounds and all talents are needed. Period.

Unfortunately, though, not everyone responds to the need. Some will ignore it; others will heed the call. For those of us who do, why exactly do we choose to get involved? Especially for those of us who aren't directly impacted by poverty in our personal lives, what's in it for us? Why should we try to become allies? Or should we?

If you've spent much time within social justice circles, you have probably seen this Australian Aboriginal saying: "If you have come to save me, you are wasting your time. But if you have come because your liberation is bound up with mine, come, let us work together." I've seen this on posters and t-shirts; it's almost becoming a cliché. Yet, in truth, it has some very profound and challenging implications, and deserves to be reflected upon carefully, not just sloganized onto a bumper sticker.

Pinpointing motivations is always tricky, because most of us approach almost everything we do out of a mix of motivations, sometimes even contradictory ones. A commitment to economic justice is no exception. We do realize that everyone's liberation is bound up together, but let's face it, it's also nice to get some kudos for doing the "right thing." After all, especially for those of us from economic privilege, one of our privileges is the option to check out of the quest for social justice. We don't have to engage. We could just pursue our individual happiness by walling ourselves off in suburban enclaves where we never have to interact with actual people living in poverty. Even those of us who are living in poverty have the option to just fight tooth and nail to get out of it and then never look back. Indeed, many people do try to ignore oppression, even their own.

Those of us, then, who are trying to pursue a different path, who are trying to create change and seeking solidarity with one another, we deserve a little credit, right? Don't we get to feel a little self-satisfied? Maybe we're not trying to be anyone's savior, but we'd at least like to be acknowledged for being on the right side of liberation.

This can quickly start to feel like a slippery slope however. If we're working for justice for our own gratification or entertainment, then are we really operating out of a spirit of mutuality and solidarity? What are the "right" reasons to work for justice? What is the "right" way to feel about our work? Is it okay to take pride in it? Is it okay to have some fun? Or should solidarity be nothing but a joyless struggle for common liberation against a merciless enemy? And why would anyone volunteer for that?

Many social activists through history have wrestled with the confusion of motivations, as well. Jane Addams, the founder of the Hull House in Chicago and one of the people most responsible for cultivating the settlement house movement and the Progressive Era political movement more broadly,[211] described both the "subjective" need for social justice efforts, and the "objective" need.[212] The objective need, she said, was the poverty and suffering so visible in society (visible, at least, to those like herself who cared to look). She worked in the slums of Chicago in the late 1800s and early 1900s. In those neighborhoods at that time, thousands of recent immigrants from Southern and Eastern Europe struggled with a lack of access to decent paying work compounded by discrimination and language barriers, and then all the social ills that followed from such poverty-stricken conditions. Many of the reforms that are now a common-sense part of our society were fought for or even pioneered at Hull House—juvenile courts, garbage collection, child labor laws, and more.[213]

So the objective need was great. But Addams also recognized the subjective need for social reform. Her subjective need was about having something stimulating and worthwhile to do as an upper-class, educated, unmarried woman at a time when professional opportunities for women were rare. Addams described the subjective needs of educated young women in terms almost as dramatic as those she used to describe the suffering in the slums: "In our attempt, then, to give a girl freedom from care we succeed, for the most part, in making her pitifully miserable... There is nothing after disease, indigence and guilt so fatal to life itself as the want of a proper outlet for active faculties."[214]

Jane had felt this want acutely herself. As a young woman in her early twenties, Jane found that her bright mind, nurtured by a high quality education, now had nothing toward which to apply itself. She became deeply depressed, and it wasn't until she conceived of the idea of Hull House and started working with some friends to implement it that she began to see more purpose in her own life and found more energy for it.[215]

Jane Addams is one of my (s)heroes and I consider her a founding foremother to a developmental tradition of allyship. But were her motivations pure? Was Jane Addams' "subjective" gain from her life of public service about pursuing her own liberation? Or was it about saving others from their "objective" need? Again, motivations are vexingly murky, but I would suspect it was some of both. She recognized how much it would expand her humanity to have a meaningful occupation, but she was also after the gratification she derived from the "moral uplift" of others, to use a phrase popular at the time.[216] Indeed that's the confusing part. The satisfaction that comes from altruistically (patronizingly?) wanting to "save" others versus the satisfaction from pursuing our own liberation can overlap and blend together and eventually become indistinguishable. So how then do we know if we are coming to save others, or coming because our liberation is bound up together?

The key is that we're measuring with the wrong metric. It's not about how much satisfaction we gain. Pursuing liberation for ourselves and for others, while challenging at times, should be a deeply satisfying and indeed joyful vocation. It is not necessarily a problem if pursuing anyone's liberation meets our subjective needs. It's okay to pat ourselves on the back once in a while for trying to be allies, especially when our allies tell us that we're living up to our intentions of working in solidarity, at least for the moment.

(Although, as a caveat, if trying to be an ally is meeting too much of our subjective needs then we're probably operating out of guilt or a false generosity as we discussed in Step Two. Further, it is not our allies' responsibility to make us feel good or assuage our guilt. They've got better things to worry about. Privileged allies need to find our own internal motivation and satisfaction.)

The problem comes if we think we are already fully liberated, and we are simply pursuing liberation entirely on someone else's behalf. Paulo Freire, in his typical blunt style, doesn't expect much good to come from those who want to liberate others and take the credit.

> Not even the best-intentioned leadership can bestow independence as a gift. The liberation of the oppressed is a liberation of women and men, not things. Accordingly, no one liberates himself by his own efforts alone, neither is he liberated by others. Liberation, a human phenomenon, cannot be achieved by semi-humans. Any attempt to treat people as semi-humans only dehumanizes them. When people are already dehumanized, due to the oppression they suffer, the process of their liberation must not employ the methods of dehumanization.[217]

If we think we can impose liberation on others from our position of enlightenment, then we are merely employing the methods of dehumanization. If we think we have all the answers to create a new society and to elevate the people in it, then we're consigning our allies to semi-human status, just the pawns in our scheme. *If you have come to save me, you are wasting your time.*

Liberation is not something we can accomplish for anyone else, working on their behalf. But, neither is it something anyone can accomplish alone. We need everyone in on this. We are all incomplete and in pursuit of our full humanity. We are all in need of assistance in pursuing our common liberation. So we <u>are</u> coming to save others, but they are saving <u>us</u> at the same time. Having the humility to recognize that will enable us to be far better allies.

Loss in liberation: Facing our fears

Even if we can start to feel a little more at ease about our motivations, we're not out of the woods yet. Recognizing our own potential for liberation may be easier to say than to do, especially for allies from economic privilege. For those of us who have benefitted from the economic status quo, there are some very real anxieties about what a "liberated" society might actually mean in material terms. What does common liberation actually look like? Who has the potential to benefit if we actually ended poverty—if we actually created an economic system where everyone has access to the resources to meet their basic needs? Who wins? Who loses?

It almost goes without saying that people currently living in poverty would gain tremendously if we were able to eliminate poverty, especially if we did so in a way that honored people's potential to contribute to society. Poverty, in my opinion, is not strictly about money. We could simply redistribute money to make sure that everyone has the same amount, or at least enough. But that wouldn't necessarily mean that everyone would then have potential to fully develop as a human being and pursue meaningful work that contributes to the broader advancement of society. That would be <u>true</u> economic justice—when everyone both has the resources they need and a way to contribute to their fullest ability toward the development of those resources. Now, we simply have vast reserves of wasted human potential. We also have people who are making significant contributions to society (by making art or raising children or building community) but are not adequately compensated or supported to do so.

As obvious as it is that people in poverty would benefit from ending poverty, it's worth pausing another moment to think just how tremendous that would be, especially on a global scale. Just like people of color are not a "minority" but in fact the global majority, people living in poverty are a global majority as well.[218] So can you imagine if all those billions of people globally no longer needed to devote most of their time and intellectual energy to survival, and instead could bring their full complement of gifts and talents into the world? How amazing would that be?

It is an inspiring possibility, but it also has the potential to make middle and owning-class people a little nervous. As much as we might not like to admit it, there are some very real ways privileged people benefit from the status quo. We often accrue gains of which we're not even aware. Herbert Gans, in his book *War on the Poor,* [219] talks about some of the functions served to society by the existence of a so-called "underclass."§ According to Gans, the privileged in society benefit by:

- Reinforcing social norms by demonizing and stigmatizing the behavior of others (often with double standards that ignore how much economically privileged people don't live up to the moral standards against which the underclass is scrutinized). "The defenders of such widely preached if not always so widely practiced values as hard work, thrift, monogamy, and moderation need people who can be accused, accurately or not, of being lazy, spendthrift, promiscuous, and dissolute... Whether or not very many poor people actually behave this way is irrelevant if they can be imagined as doing so."[220]

- Psychologically distancing themselves from the "underclass," which allows them to avoid perceived risks of criminality, and to have a scapegoat for social fears and moral anxieties.

- Developing a supply system for illegal goods, like drugs, out of view of the "respectable" neighborhoods of many of the people who actually use those illegal goods.

- Scapegoating the poor to reduce attention to the inadequacies and ineffectiveness of institutions or markets claiming to promote social progress, like schools, the housing market, or the healthcare system.

---

§ Consistent with Gans' usage, I am using the term "underclass" not because we believe that people struggling with poverty truly are an underclass, but to denote how they are unfairly understood by many in broader society and portrayed in the media.

- Delegitimizing the political demands or political power of low-wealth people or anyone who supports their demands, which allows politicians of all parties to focus more on the needs of upper-class constituents and businesses.

- Supplying a reserve army of labor to keep downward pressure on wages and keep costs low.

- Removing a large segment of potential competition out of the labor force. This is accomplished largely through the criminalization of poverty (for instance, through disproportionately harsh sentences for non-violent drug offenses, or the increased police surveillance of poor communities), and the subsequent collateral consequences to individuals in the labor market.

- Gaining jobs in the "helping professions," and gaining outlets for charity and volunteer energy. As Gans states, "It could be argued that some of the rules for handling the undeserving poor are more effective at performing the latent function of creating jobs for the working and middle classes than achieving their stated goals of enforcing the laws."[221]

This is not a flattering list. Now, before we move on to address it, it should be noted that Gans describes these as "functions" of an underclass, and explicitly states that "functions are not purposes. They are not what people intend to do, but are the consequences of what they actually do, whatever their initial purposes."[222] So these functions should not necessarily be assumed to be some evil, intentional plot of the elites. However, Gans also states that once people begin to receive the benefits of these functions, they may subconsciously or consciously seek to preserve them.

If those of us with economic privilege who are seeking solidarity with those living in poverty have all of this to gain by the continued existence of poverty, can we honestly say that we are invested in ending it? Can we really see the light at the end of this tunnel, a light representing our own potential for liberation?

I certainly hope so. Because to me, the very ugliness of this list of "functions"—the fear, the pettiness, the anxiety over scarcity, the blaming, the judgment—makes them prime candidates for things from which we should want to be liberated. Once again, Paulo Freire has wise words to share, which we saw already in Step Two but deserve to be repeated: "As the oppressors dehumanize others and violate their rights, they themselves also become dehumanized. As the oppressed, fighting to be human, take away the oppressors' power to dominate and suppress, they restore to the oppressors the humanity they had lost in the exercise of oppression."[223] For those of us from economic privilege, part of our liberation will involve no longer needing to scapegoat, stigmatize, or subjugate.

Even though we know that ending poverty will help restore our humanity, it will still help us to be better allies if we can be honest about what we might lose, or even what we just fear that we might lose from our position of economic privilege. By bringing these fears out into the light, we can expose them for the fallacies they are. And we can better prevent them from operating beyond our conscious awareness to subvert our attempts at solidarity.

For me personally, one fear that I've had is about losing my sense of purpose. I worked for a few years at a job where I didn't feel much of a sense of mission in the world, and it was rough. It was a decent job in terms of pay and benefits (in fact, better than the two subsequent jobs I would go on to take in the poverty industry), the people I worked with were nice, and I felt the company was ethical and producing a quality product. But despite all that, nearly every week, by about Thursday evening I would be strung out, exhausted and frustrated. My husband and I even coined the term "Thursday Funk" because the pattern was so predictable. The problem wasn't just that the job was stressful but that the stress didn't serve any broader purpose. Did it really even matter in the bigger scheme of things if a retailer purchased our product over a competitor's? Why was I so stressed out about trade shows or catalog printings? Why was I investing so much time and energy into this?

This is not to put down business people. Many people make an honest and ethical living in business and we need those people to produce the necessaries (and some of the pleasures) of everyday life. But for me, when I wasn't able to connect to a sense of purpose, the work became wearisome. Since leaving that job, I have had the good fortune to do work with much more meaning and consequence. I get to help develop the strengths of others and see their growth and progress on a daily basis. I get to provide valuable assistance to people who really need it. I get to make a significant positive impact on the lives of others. As a result of these experiences, I've invested much of my professional and personal identity into helping others, and specifically in working with individuals in generational poverty. That's my subjective need. So how would I find my purpose and satisfaction if poverty was gone and my "clients" no longer "needed" me?

I don't want my subjective need for purpose in my work to overshadow my interest in economic liberation for myself and the families I work with—common liberation that in the long run would be in the best interest of us both. One exercise that I've used to restrain my more selfish interests is to envision that exact scenario. What if poverty was gone? Can I picture society as it would be? [224] What would I do? My fantasy is that I would run a muffin shop, where I would sell tasty and wholesome pastries to my neighborhood. I can even picture the shop—inviting décor with lots of warm wood, a few comfy couches, indoor plants, probably an outdoor patio/garden... I can smell it in my imagination as well—one of the best smells in the world, I think. And my welcoming, beautiful, fragrant muffin shop would be a hub for friends and groups to connect with one another and enjoy each other's company.

So, in the unlikely event that we end poverty in my lifetime, I have a plan. Maybe it's even a vision that I will integrate into my social justice work someday. I could at least start by baking muffins for my allies a bit more often. Seriously, though, this little thought exercise helps me stay invested in the dream of common liberation. What is your plan for a future society? What would you do?

We are the 99%: Inequality and inclusion

The problems in rich countries are not caused by the society not being rich enough (or even by being too rich) but by the scale of material differences between people within each society being too big. What matters is where we stand in relation to others in our own society.

-Richard Wilkinson and Kate Pickett[225]

The benefits of a more just society don't all have to be hypothetical, however. Nor do they belong to any one class, exclusively. One of the biggest benefits of ending poverty is that it would bring about a more economically equal society overall, which has great potential to benefit everyone.

In their book *The Spirit Level: Why Greater Equality Makes Societies Stronger,* Richard Wilkinson and Kate Pickett analyze a vast body of research into social inequality and its correlation to a host of negative social outcomes.[226] They find that higher degrees of income inequality are correlated with poorer mental health outcomes, higher degrees of drug use, worse physical health and life expectancy, more disparate educational performance, more violence, higher rates of incarceration, and, perhaps worst of all, less social mobility, setting up a downward spiral. They found consistent patterns when comparing states across the US, as well as internationally among developed countries. Income inequalities seemed to be associated with some very stark differences in well-being, even within many of the most prosperous societies in the world.

In their research, Wilkinson and Pickett took care to rule out other plausible explanations for the patterns they observed. The most obvious alternative explanation would be the assumption that higher incomes directly correlate to better social outcomes. Thereby, more unequal societies, with presumably lower overall incomes dragged down by poorer poor, had worse outcomes. This didn't turn out to be the case for a couple reasons. First, overall income is correlated with better social outcomes—to a point.[227] Data shows that on a global scale, there is a pattern of diminishing returns where continued increases in income produce smaller and smaller gains in other positive measures. The authors argue that most developed countries, where the per capita income is plenty sufficient to meet basic needs, have reached a leveling off point where continued increases in income will not make much difference in long-term health or well-being indicators on a societal level.

Plus, not only does income seem to make less difference in developed nations, it's also the case that inequality is the far better predictor of social outcomes.[228] In fact, among the countries included, the highest and the lowest countries in overall income were worst and second worst, respectively, on a general health and social problems scale. These two countries, the United States and Portugal, had a great difference in per capita income, but a great similarity in degree of inequality. By contrast, the countries that scored the best on social outcomes, Japan and Sweden, were middle of the road income-wise, but both very low-inequality. So inequality of income is capturing some social dynamic distinct from the amount of income alone.

Another assumption might be that the higher incidence of social problems in highly unequal societies is simply related to social dysfunction among the bottom strata of society. But research doesn't support this assumption either. The scale of differences is so vast that the issues are affecting nearly everyone in highly unequal societies, including the privileged. Health and longevity differences are a telling example:

> The effects of inequality are not confined just to the least well-off: instead they affect the vast majority of the population. To take an example, the reason why life expectancy is 4.5 years shorter for the average American than it is for the average Japanese, is not primarily because the poorest 10 percent of Americans suffer a life expectancy deficit ten times as large (i.e. forty-five years) while the rest of the population does as well as the Japanese. As epidemiologist Michael Marmot frequently points out, you could take away all the health problems of the poor and still leave most of the problem of health inequalities untouched.[229]

In other words, while health inequality by class is a real problem in the United States, we are all doing less well than the Japanese.

Why does inequality seem to have such a strong influence on so many aspects of human life for everyone across the income spectrum? While we can't be entirely sure of the direction of causation in these statistics, Wilkinson and Pickett speculate that much of the negative impact of inequality stems from the stresses and anxieties of social comparison.[230] When social differences are heightened, one's relative lack is very obvious, even if it's the top 10% comparing themselves to the top 1%. Or as we saw in Step Three, even if it's a homeless mother on welfare comparing herself to another with an apartment. These comparisons are painful, they erode our sense of self-worth, and they often pit us against one another. Greater social comparison can even be associated with greater degrees of violence and aggression. "When people react to a provocation from someone with higher status by redirecting their aggression on to someone of lower status, psychologists label it *displaced aggression.* Examples include: the man who is berated by his boss and comes home and shouts at his wife and children; the higher degree of aggression in workplaces where supervisors treat workers unfairly; the ways in which people in deprived communities react to an influx of foreign immigrants."[231] Another form of displaced aggression is, as Gans pointed out, the twisted satisfaction of scapegoating the poor for the kinds of social problems associated with inequality.[232] Social distancing does not bring out our best as human beings.

Further, when social mobility is limited, but the praising of the mega-rich is ubiquitous, people will resort to more and more drastic measures to shore up their sense of status and pride—whether they try to buy it, exploit or put down others to get it, or physically harm anyone who threatens it. All of this further weakens social cohesion and trust, which is then itself another source of stress taking its toll on our health.

High degrees of inequality can also make us less comfortable with the resources that we do have. Honestly, a certain level of discomfort may sometimes be appropriate. I remember once participating in an activity about global wealth distribution. A commodity—I believe it was rice grains, in this case—was distributed to the people in the room proportionally to the actual wealth distribution of the world. As you can imagine, most of us got one grain of rice, and really only one person had a proper bowlful. Then we were read a series of statistics such that if there were 100 people in the world, only one would own a computer, a much higher number would be malnourished, and so forth.[233] In this hypothetical global village, it seemed perfectly obvious that the one person sitting there with his computer and bowl full of rice would obviously share it with everyone else. After all, we other 99 hungry people were right here in front of him! How could he live with himself if he didn't share?

This was the intended moral lesson of this activity, of course. But when poverty is distributed across billions of people on multiple continents, it's not quite as obvious that the rice misers will share, or even how they would go about it. Even so, the question remains. For those of us with more than enough, how can we live with ourselves if we don't share it?

I said earlier that one of the privileges of economic privilege is that we can choose to live ignorantly and detachedly from inequality and poverty. But that's not entirely true. As much as we might try to insulate ourselves from the economic realities, we can never totally shut it out. As we've just learned, even if we could avoid any awareness of poverty, the unhealthy effects of inequality will shorten our lives and decrease our life satisfaction as well. And we also can't totally ignore the suffering poverty causes for others. We will still encounter people dealing with poverty as we go about our daily lives, if nothing else because their inadequately paying service jobs subsidize our lifestyles.[234] We'll also see poverty in our political debates, and in the media, and even a few rare occasions when people living in poverty manage to get to the podium long enough to speak for themselves about their lives and their aspirations and needs. So one of the burdens of a grossly unequal and unjust society is a certain unavoidable guilt. As we discussed in Step Two, guilt and shame does not make for a healthy foundation of allyship relationships, so we don't want to wallow in our guilt about the current system. But a more just and equal economy could liberate us from even the potential to feel guilty. If we were part of a fair economy, we could enjoy the resources we have more, knowing they were fairly earned.

A more fair economy might also be one in which we could be more trusting of one another, and less apt to be so bitterly divided by demographic or political differences. Some people have tried to marshal that sense of solidarity as an antidote to the high degree of inequality in our society. The Occupy Wall Street movement popularized the slogan "We are the 99%," which aimed to help the vast majority of Americans recognize their common economic interests—interests presumed to be counter to the tiny 1% minority that controls <u>4,440 times</u> more wealth than the bottom 40% of Americans.[235] That top 1%, vastly over-represented among our politicians (of both parties) and other power-brokers, has seen their share of income and wealth continue to rise right off the charts, and have enacted business and tax policies that seem to ensure the continuation of that trend.

Many people believe that the elite 1% very intentionally exploits the differences between the other 99% of us and pits us against one another to secure their own political dominance. I don't doubt that has been true at times. History is full of examples of groups seeking political gain by exploiting one faction over another and setting up conflicts and distractions. But I also personally believe that a resistance based on divisions, even the 99% versus the 1%, isn't the best answer. *The work of ending poverty will require the gifts and talents of everyone, no matter what class background they come from.* I'd rather work with everyone who recognizes how they truly stand to gain from a more just society, whether they come from the bottom 5th percentile, the 42nd percentile, or the 99.9[th]. (Although I would certainly ask the 99.9[th] percentile ally to share some resources for the cause!) I believe that a movement to end poverty that is based on a positive vision of a better society will be more effective than one based solely on opposition to the status quo.

For similar reasons, I think it is important not to have any political litmus test for our allies. We can certainly debate about politics, and can and should be involved in the political sphere. But neither political party in the United States, nor even political parties in the more egalitarian societies like

Sweden and Japan, have totally figured out how to eliminate poverty and create real economic opportunity for everyone.

I personally tend to get a little tired of the same old policy prescriptions that get trotted out by both political parties. Democrats emphasize redistribution and social services, and Republicans emphasize business de-regulation and personal responsibility. It seems to me that there ought to be more creative solutions to poverty, inequality and economic growth. For one thing, we get so stuck on the same tedious debates about redistribution. Will it create opportunity or dependency? Is it fair to take money earned by one person to give it to another? Is it right for the 1% to amass so much wealth without contributing to the commons? Spinning around on these same monotonous questions ignores the possibility of creating a better system of <u>distribution</u> in the first place, so less <u>re</u>-distribution would even be necessary. We don't have to "take away" money from anyone to "give" it to someone else if we make sure that everyone has fair access to earn it in the first place. But we get stuck in the well-worn grooves of capitalism, since it's the only successful economic system most of us have ever known. And our political system takes the market economy as a given and feeds its needs. As William Greider has said, "the efforts of government have always fallen short of what is needed. They have not, and perhaps cannot, overcome the originating sources within capitalism of our injury. They have contained it in various ways—they have domesticated it. But the system is still with us."[236]

As you can see, my personal political stance is a fairly radical one that is not well represented by any mainstream politicians. But I am not against working with allies who support any (or no) political parties. I think conservatives have some good principles and liberals do too. By working in solidarity, and by including the many who have felt disengaged and disheartened by our existing political systems, we will come up with novel solutions that transcend traditional political boundaries. Hopefully then we can create a fair economy that engages 100% of our society with meaningful work and a fair distribution of resources.

That kind of economic system would be truly liberatory for everyone involved. Everyone could earn a fair share and feel fully justified in what they earn. Without vast inequalities in wealth, we would all feel more satisfied with what we do have, and willing to invest more time and effort in the non-monetary things of value—family, community, creative pursuits, maintaining beautiful and healthy natural environments to be enjoyed in common. I believe such a society is possible. And I believe that we are all needed to work together, to combine our unique gifts, in action and in reflection, to define what that society will look like and how it will come to be.

Conclusion: Solidarity and Hope

Novice: 1. A person who is new to the circumstances, work, etc. in which he or she is placed; beginner

- Random House Dictionary[237]

The revolution is made neither by the leaders for the people nor by the people for the leaders, but by both acting together in unshakable solidarity. This solidarity is born only when the leaders witness to it by their humble, loving and courageous encounter with the people. Not all men and women have sufficient courage for this encounter.

- Paulo Freire[238]

In the years since the Allyship Project did our work together, there has been a growing school of thought critical of the concept and word "ally."[239] Before I conclude, I'd like to address some of the critiques very directly.

To begin with, I should note that they usually define allyship differently than the Allyship Project did. Namely, these authors use the term "ally" as it is most often used: to refer exclusively to allies from privilege. By contrast, as you recall, our group felt that people from <u>all</u> class backgrounds had the potential to be allies to one another in the work to create a more just society, so we created a more inclusive definition. Even so, throughout this book we've been discussing many dynamics and responsibilities that are specific to middle-class and owning-class allies, and in the following discussion we will shift the definition of "ally" to the more conventional, exclusive one.

The critiques of allyship have some common themes and shared frustrations. The exasperation stems primarily from encountering people who are claiming to be allies but are not living up to the potential of allyship. Usually this is in the context of white allies working with people of color, but I'm sure the same dynamics can and do play out in mixed class groups. Some of the most prominent concerns are:

- Allies take up an identity as an ally, whether or not their behavior warrants it.

  This is problematic in multiple ways. First of all, allyship is an action, not an identity. According to Mia McKenzie, "'Ally' cannot be a label that someone stamps onto you— or, god forbid, that you stamp on to yourself—so you can then go around claiming it as some kind of identity. It's not an identity. It's a practice. It's an active thing that must be done over and over again, in the largest and smallest ways, every day."[240]

  Even worse, sometimes allies will defend hurtful statements or actions by saying, "It's okay. I'm an ally."[241] Not only does this excuse not make any sense if "ally" is supposed to be an action, but also a true ally should be willing to examine and change their behavior if it hurts someone else, regardless of the original intention.

Secondly, when an ally is someone outside an oppressed community helping someone who's inside and that becomes a core feature of the ally's identity, it crystalizes and exaggerates a distinction between I and Other. Our relationships become rigidly defined by stereotyped roles: I am The Middle-class Ally and you are The Poor. In reality, most of us exist in multiple identities, some of which experience oppression and some of which experience privilege.[242] Plus, we all experience and internalize our unique combinations of oppression and privilege in different ways. Therefore, even as allies try to learn about cultural distinctions and respect people's cultural identities, we run the risk of reducing unique individuals to just identities and stereotypes.

- Allies let go of personal responsibility for their behavior because they are following leaders of oppressed communities

According to M., an activist in North Carolina:

> A good ally learns that if you can never understand the implications of walking through this world as an oppressed [fill in the blank with a person on the receiving end of a specific oppression], the only way to act with integrity is to follow the leadership of those who are oppressed in that way, support their projects and their goals, and always seek out their suggestions and listen to their ideas when you are not sure what to do next. [243]

Taken to the extreme, this means that an ally abdicates any and all personal responsibility for deciding their own actions, or developing or defending their own thoughts. This extreme passivity makes an ally into a "wimpy wannabe" ally, not helpful to anyone.[244] Or an ally may roar around like a bull in a china shop, accusing people of being oppressive or inciting dangerous situations, but admitting no responsibility because they are acting "on behalf of" an oppressed community.

There is also the unavoidable reality that oppressed communities are not monolithic.[245] People in poverty (or people of color, or women, etc.) have widely varying and sometimes opposing political beliefs, religious traditions, cultural practices, etc. So even as we develop relationships across class boundaries and seek to educate ourselves by listening to people who have directly experienced oppression, we still cannot assume that our teachers speak for all people who have ever experienced that oppression.

- Allies act in ways that dominate or suppress the leadership of oppressed communities

One critic describes the "ally industrial complex" as careerist allies who move in on activist groups and communities and impose their "allyship" without earning the consent and trust of those communities.[246] They will try to take over the agenda or seek attention and notoriety if they think it can further their reputation and career. And they certainly cannot be counted on to stick around long enough to help deal with any consequences of their actions.

Sometimes allies seem to feel that their "allyness" has earned them the right to forcefully impose their views and goals on others, even if that runs exactly counter to the ethic of being an ally in the first place. "Is it because when we feel like we occupy the most legitimate or objectively most justified position (often according to a strangely quantitative evaluation of those who are most wronged by social oppressions), it is easy to inflate our sense of righteousness?" asks M.[247] M goes on to tell stories of people advocating for peace who will violently restrain fellow protesters whose behavior they dislike, or white allies who will insert themselves into a disagreement and shout insults at people of color.   An inflated sense of righteousness indeed.

- Allies seek a lot of emotional energy and support from oppressed communities to learn / process / make themselves feel better about their privilege

We've already seen a vivid example of a white "ally" intruding on a space meant to be reserved as a safe space people of color, primarily because she wanted to apologize and seek absolution.[248] (See Step Seven). This happens over and over again, in smaller, less egregious ways, but consistently enough to be pretty exhausting for people who have to deal with it. Especially because they're already exhausted from dealing with the oppression itself. "We must not get so caught up in our own self-discoveries that we unthinkingly put the emotional weight of those breakthrough moments on others who live daily with the realities we are just beginning to understand," writes M.[249] If people living with classism or racism or other -ism's help us out by supporting and educating us, we can be extremely grateful. But it's not fair to always expect them to.

This phenomenon is worsened exponentially when the emotional processing is motivated by guilt or shame. "Guilt is also a primary ally motivating factor," writes one anonymous commentator writing from an 'indigenous perspective.'

> While guilt and shame are powerful emotions, think about what you're doing before you make another community's struggle into your therapy session. Of course, acts of resistance and liberation can be quite healing, but tackling guilt, shame, and other trauma requires a much different focus, or at least an explicit and consensual focus. What kind of relationships are built on guilt and shame?[250]

After experiencing all of the above multiple times, Mia McKenzie finally declared, "Allyship is not supposed to look like this, folks. It's not supposed to be about you. It's not supposed to be about your feelings. It's not supposed to be a way of glorifying yourself at the expense of the folks you claim to be an ally to. It's not supposed to be a performance."[251] She decides she's not even going to use the word "ally" any more. Her alternative is "currently operating in solidarity with..." which she admits is "clunky as hell."[252] Other thinkers suggest the terms "accomplice" or "affinity." But in all cases, they're pretty fed up with "allies."

I hear the deep pain and frustration in these polemics. And I realize that by continuing to use the word "ally," I'm running the risk of the same kind of entitlement that frustrates them. By sticking with the term "ally" and naming myself as someone trying to be one, am I simply asserting my privilege yet again?

I hope not. But why do I remain with the word at all? There are a couple of reasons. First, on a very pragmatic level, the Allyship Project was the Allyship Project, not the Solidarity Project, or the Mutual Aid Project, or any other term. We worked long and hard on our definition of "ally," and because we fundamentally shifted allyship to include everyone, I think our definition already challenged a few of the problematic parts of the traditional allyship model. So, although thinking can and should change and evolve (and indeed some members of the Allyship group may be more likely to use other terms today), I wanted in this book to represent our work as it actually was, while at the same time incorporating related concepts and experiences that have informed my thinking since.

Secondly, and probably most importantly, I believe that most of the criticisms of "allies" are criticisms that I would fully share, and in fact have shared in these pages. My hope is that my concept of what makes for a good ally (or, rather, someone attempting to be one) is essentially the same as the meaning of "currently operating in solidarity." I agree that someone seeking to stand in solidarity should never stop actively working to support their allies. I agree that allies should recognize their own personal stake in seeking liberation, and own their personal contributions toward that effort. I agree that operating in solidarity means not replicating oppressive patterns of exerting leadership over others, or stereotyping and making assumptions about others. I agree that allies should take responsibility for their own learning and processing. I agree with M. that:

> Recognizing the autonomy and self-determination of individuals and groups acknowledges their capability. It's an understanding of that group as having something of worth to be gained through interactions with them, whether that thing is a material good or something less tangible, like perspective, joy or inspiration. The solidarity model dispels the idea of one inside and one outside, foregrounding how individuals belong to multiple groups and how groups overlap with one another, while simultaneously demanding respect for the identity and self-sufficiency of each of those groups.[253]

I believe that this is the true promise of solidarity and allyship, when practiced as it's meant to be. So I hope the disagreement is less about substance than semantics.

Then why not just adjust my own language, if it's just semantics? Aside from wanting to respect the history of the Allyship Project, my other concern is that the language proposed as alternatives doesn't feel quite right to me. I haven't come across a term that I like enough to completely replace "ally" or "allyship." "Currently operating in solidarity with …" is specific, but it is clunky as hell as its author admitted, and the "with…" on the end leaves in place the I-versus-Other distinction of traditional allyship.

Also, "solidarity" often gets paired with the verb "to stand." Standing in solidarity sounds motionless and inert to me. Isn't it just as easy for me to declare myself as "in solidarity" with whomever I choose as it would be to declare myself their "ally?" In fact, ally sounds to me <u>more</u> active and purposeful, and also more mutual. Allies enter into conflicts with one another, fight alongside one another, and recognize their mutual need for support. In that vein, some have suggested "accomplice" as an alternative term, but that is a bit more aggressive than I'm ready to be.

My hope is that as the language evolves, we may find new words to describe our partnerships and collaborations that are even more descriptive and appropriate. In the meantime, while I have looked for opportunities throughout this book to incorporate "solidarity" and to emphasize the verb-ness of "ally," I am still stubbornly sticking to the term. I've chosen to try to define allyship in my own way, informed by the collaborative work of my allies, and in so doing to hopefully reclaim the word from those who have misapplied it.

Even as I claim the word, I do not wish to claim "ally" as an identity. This is one of the points on which I totally agree with the critics. Those of us seeking to be allies don't get to decide when we've gotten there. There's no finish line to cross; there's no badge to be earned and sewn on our vest. Becoming an ally, or seeking to act in solidarity, is not something we will ever complete, nor is it something we get to claim for ourselves. Only our allies can decide whether or not we are living up to the true meaning of the term, and only for the time being.

I actually find that more hopeful than daunting. It's okay to be a novice, because we are all learning this new way of being together. And we all have the potential to continually improve our relationships with one another, our knowledge of ourselves, and our collective capacity to bring about our common liberation. We also have many mentors from whom to learn, both living and those who have gone before. While the developmental tradition may not have a name, it is there.[254] It is a long and venerable tradition of people who have recognized that they could work in partnership with others to create a more just society and economy that gives all people a legitimate opportunity for prosperity, in more than just financial terms. It is a tradition I hope to join, and this book is my small attempt to share what I have learned on that journey thus far.

Reasons for hope

I have read many books on many different subjects that have one thing in common. The author will spend pages and pages, chapter after chapter, analyzing and diagnosing a problem. Then in the conclusion, there is inevitably some rather anemic statement that the author hopes the book will "start a conversation" about how the problem might be addressed. I always feel a little let down when I get to that line of the conclusion. I'm left wanting more. I read the pages that led up to that point usually because they addressed an issue I'd like to approach in a new way—a problem I want to do something about, not just know more about. I want a more impactful next step than just conversing.

Sometimes those kinds of analyses actually do start important conversations. Nevertheless, I hope I have not written that sort of book here, nor that sort of conclusion. I hope you have found a call for action (and reflection). As imperfect and incomplete as I'm sure they are, I hope you have come away with some concrete suggestions for how to put allyship into actual practice, how to operate in solidarity. And I hope you feel more hopeful about your capacity to attempt to be an effective ally.

I feel that I am still very much a novice at this effort. I'm sure my understanding will deepen as I seek to live out the principles I've outlined. And I'm sure some of those principles will shift and change as I gain more experience. I'm also confident that I will fail, more than once, to live up to my own goals. I hope I've avoided too much self-righteousness, even as I have tried to give actionable instructions. None of my directives are here because they are skills I have fully mastered—they are here because I was seeking instructions for my own efforts to be a better ally, and still am. But I am hopeful that I can keep learning and hopeful I can be a benefit to my allies.

Tony Kushner once said that being hopeful is a responsibility:

> You don't look at [hope] as a feeling state; you look at it as an ethical obligation. You look at it as a thing that you generate in yourself by recognizing that despair is a luxury. Not for everyone. Some people are really burdened by life, either because of chemicals in their brains or terrible personal circumstances or social circumstances that make despair inescapable. But most people in this country aren't. And since most of us aren't, we have an ethical obligation to look for hope and find it. It isn't easy, but that doesn't mean it isn't there. In fact, if it were easy, it would be less valuable. It's like the Jewish search for God. One of the Talmudic ideas for why it's so hard is that you create its value by the difficulty of the search. We all do it. That's what our struggle is. We wouldn't get out of bed otherwise. [255]

I love that concept. I had always thought of hope as something bestowed by the universe; something you either had or you didn't. But for most of us, hope is actually an obligation. It is something we must cultivate, for our own health and to share with others. I find my greatest hope in my allies. I find hope in the allies who've radiated love and care for all those around them, including me. The allies who've marched in the streets and demanded something new. The allies who've written books or spoken poems to help me learn. The allies who've challenged me with deep conversations. The allies who've dedicated lives and professions to helping others, recognizing that they've gained as much toward their own liberation as they've given.

I know there are amazing people with beautiful hearts doing creative things to make positive changes, even if their voices sometimes get drowned out by the more oppressive elements of our society. But when I've looked intently for allies, I've found them. When I've listened carefully for the hidden tradition, I've heard it. When I've needed support and love, I've felt it. So I chose to have hope. I choose to believe that ending poverty is possible, because I've met too many humans, from all backgrounds, who are better than that. We're all better than that. So I hope that we can find solidarity with one another to create a new way.

Further Reading

This is by no means a comprehensive list, but here are some of the thinkers and storytellers who have been influential for me.

First-hand accounts and analysis from people who have lived in poverty

Julia Dinsmore: *My Name is Child of God, Not "Those People": A First-Person Look at Poverty.* Minneapolis: Augsburg Fortress. (2007).

Donna M. Beegle: *See Poverty... Be the Difference! Discover the Missing Pieces for Helping People Move Out of Poverty.* Tigard, OR: Communication Across Barriers. (2007).

Linda Stout: *Bridging the Class Divide and other Lessons for Grassroots Organizing.* Boston: Beacon. (1996).

Theresa Funiciello: *Tyranny of Kindness: Dismantling the Welfare System to End Poverty in America.* New York: Atlantic Monthly. (1993).

Class analysis and allyship theory

Paulo Freire: *Pedagogy of the Oppressed,* 30th anniversary edition. New York: Continuum. (1970/2009).

Myles Horton & Paulo Freire: *We Make the Road by Walking: Conversations on Education and Social Change.* (Editors) B. Bell, J. Gaventa, & J. Peters. Philadelphia: Temple University Press. (1990).

Mary Field Belenky, Lynne A. Bond, & Jacqueline S. Weinstock: *A Tradition that Has No Name: Nurturing the Development of People, Families, and Communities.* New York: Basic Books. (1997).

Betsy Leondar-Wright: *Class Matters: Cross-Class Alliance Building for Middle Class Activists.* Gabriola Island, BC: New Society. (2005).

Mia McKenzie: *Black Girl Dangerous: On Race, Queerness, Class and Gender.* Oakland, CA: BGD (2014).

bell hooks: *Where We Stand: Class Matters.* New York: Routledge. (2000).

Michael B. Katz: *The Undeserving Poor: America's Enduring Confrontation with Poverty* (2nd Ed.) Oxford, UK: Oxford. (2013).

Francesca Ramsey: "5 Tips for Being an Ally." Video: https://youtu.be/_dg86g-QlMO (2014).

Stories about poverty from privileged allies

Robert Putnam: *Our Kids: The American Dream in Crisis.* New York: Simon & Schuster. (2015).

Edin, K. and M. Kefalas. *Promises I Can Keep: Why Poor Women Put Motherhood Before Marriage.* Berkeley: University of California Press. (2005).

Father Gregory Boyle: *Tattoos on the Heart: The Power of Boundless Compassion.* New York, NY: Free Press. (2010).

Barbara Ehrenreich: *Nickel and Dimed: On (Not) Getting By in America.* New York, NY: Henry Holt. (2001).

Appendix I: Seven Steps to Becoming a Better Ally

The following steps were written collaboratively by the Allyship Project: a cross-class partnership of anti-poverty activists. From 2010-2012, the Allyship Project explored how to be better allies in our relationships with people who came from different class backgrounds than ourselves. Members included legislative advocates, a spoken-word poetry artist, a radio show host, social service workers, and mothers and grandmothers. The Allyship Project worked with A Minnesota Without Poverty to develop a series of trainings targeted to middle/owning- class allies.

Definition of an ally

An ally is a person who seeks to end poverty, and who partners with people from all class backgrounds to work toward that goal.

An ally develops personal, responsible, respectful and mutually beneficial relationships with people from different class backgrounds than him/herself. These relationships are not necessarily friendships, but are at least respectful working relationships bound together by a common goal of ending poverty.

Seven steps to becoming a better ally

Step 1: Educate Yourself on the Realities of Poverty

An ally should try to learn as much as possible directly from members of communities that have experienced poverty, allowing them to speak in their own words rather than only through economically privileged "experts". At the same time, an ally takes responsibility for her own learning and does not passively wait to be "educated" by people living in poverty.

Step 2: Educate Yourself on Oppression and Privilege in Our Society. Examine How You May Have Internalized Oppression and/or Privilege That You Have Experienced

Everyone in our society has been exposed to stereotypes and misinformation about ourselves and others. An ally should always be on the lookout for ways in which he may have come to believe these lies, consciously or unconsciously, and challenge that internalization in himself.

Step 3: Explore How Internalized Oppression or Privilege May Affect Your Behavior in Cross-Class Relationships

For example, sometimes people who have internalized privilege believe that due to their education and experience, their ideas and suggestions will always be superior to people who have less education. They may begin to think of people in poverty as less intelligent or less informed, and not consider their ideas seriously. This may happen at an unconscious level, even though the person consciously believes that everyone's ideas are important.

If an ally is experiencing a confusing conflict with people from a different class background, the ally should first consider whether internalized oppression or privilege might be contributing to the conflict.

Step 4: Seek Out Opportunities to Be in Mutually Beneficial Relationships with People from a Different Class Background than Yourself

Look for opportunities where people are working together on a common goal, and power and leadership is shared. Find and appreciate "bridge people" who have authentic connections in multiple communities and can help make introductions and facilitate relationship building. These should be relationships other than service provider/client, donor/recipient, or advocate/victim.

Step 5: Seek Out Opportunities to Support the Leadership of People Who Have Lived or Are Living in Poverty

Due to social and economic oppression, people in poverty are rarely given positions of significant leadership. Part of the work of ending poverty is reversing this pattern, starting in our own social change efforts. So it is of utmost importance that an ally respects the leadership of groups and individuals who have experienced long-term poverty, and supports their self-determination and self-efficacy. An ally who is economically privileged should as much as possible try to not exert power over the decision making of people from less privileged backgrounds.

Step 6: Respect the Inherent Human Dignity and Cultural Values and Practices of Everyone

An ally recognizes that no one should be required to fundamentally deny or change their culture in order to achieve economic opportunity. An ally who is economically privileged must be careful not to assume that all people living in poverty want to "be like them" or "look like them." She should not impose her cultural values or practices during the struggle for economic rights and opportunity.

Step 7: Recognize the Unique Contributions That You Can Make to the Common Purpose of Ending Poverty

No human liberation movement in the history of humankind has ever progressed without allies. So the work of ending poverty will require the gifts and talents of everyone, no matter what class background they come from.

Appendix II: Allyship Project Mission & Vision Statements

Allyship Project Mission Statement

The Allyship Project teaches methods of building principled partnerships across the class divide, grounding the work to end poverty in the practical change and real wisdom of low-wealth leaders.

Allyship Project Vision Statement

The Allyship Project envisions a society that has achieved economic liberation for all people, where poverty does not exist. We believe that to accomplish this, people from all class backgrounds must work together, because no human liberation movement has ever succeeded without developing allies. We will empower the groups and organizations we work with to transcend old models of interaction across class such as academia study, evangelical missionary work, or social services exploitation. Instead, we will help them implement a new model for forming relationships across the class divide which are personal, responsible and mutually beneficial, so all people can work effectively together to liberate ourselves from poverty.

The Allyship Project is also committed to making space for the all-too-often invisible and under-valued gifts, strengths, and talents of low-wealth citizens. It is indeed time that poor people are integrally involved in creating solutions that result in our own liberation. In safety and in unity we overcome the internalized oppression of generational poverty, we build community and we develop our leadership.

- Saint Paul, Minnesota (2011)

Notes and References

---

[1] Freire, P. (1970/2009). *Pedagogy of the Oppressed,* 30th anniversary ed. New York: Continuum. p. 60-61

[2] Belenky, M. F., L. A. Bond, & J. S. Weinstock (1997). *A Tradition that Has No Name: Nurturing the Development of People, Families, and Communities.* New York: Basic Books. p. 293

[3] Ibid p. 258 - 292

[4] Toynbee Hall is widely credited as the original settlement house, and the one that inspired Jane Addams to create the Hull House in Chicago. It could be said that Toynbee is a spiritual birthplace of the modern tradition that has no name. See: Knight, L. W. (2005). *Citizen: Jane Addams and the Struggle for Democracy.* Chicago: U of Chicago. p. 166-185; and Belenky, M. F., L. A. Bond, & J. S. Weinstock (1997). *A Tradition that Has No Name: Nurturing the Development of People, Families, and Communities.* New York: Basic Books. p. 175-176.

[5] Bishop, A.. "Becoming an Ally: Tools for Achieving Equity in People and Institutions." Retrieved Sept. 4, 2017 from: http://www.becominganally.ca/ Becoming an Ally/Home.html. See also Bishop, A. (2002). *Becoming an Ally: Breaking the Cycle of Oppression in People.* (2nd Ed) London, UK: Zed.

[6] For instance, Kivel, P. (2002). *How White People Can Work for Racial Justice.* Gabriola Island, BC: New Society; or Wise, T. (2011). *White Like Me: Reflections on Race from a Privileged Son,* Berkeley, CA: Soft Skull Press.

[7] For instance, hooks, b. (2000). *Feminism is for Everybody: Passionate Politics.* Boston, MA: South End.

[8] For instance, Hall, D. M. (2009). *Allies at Work: Creating a Lesbian, Gay, Bisexual and Transgender Inclusive Work Environment.* San Francisco, CA: Out & Equal.

[9] There are a few excellent resources on the topic. A few I recommend include: Leondar-Wright, B. (2005). *Class Matters: Cross-Class Alliance Building for Middle Class Activists.* Gabriola Island, BC: New Society; Stout, L. (1996). *Bridging the Class Divide and other Lessons for Grassroots Organizing.* Boston: Beacon; Bishop, A. (2002). *Becoming an Ally: Breaking the Cycle of Oppression in People.* (2nd Ed) London, UK: Zed.

[10] For example: M. (Feb. 7, 2015). "A Critique of Ally Politics."Retrieved from: https://radicalwashtenaw.org/2015/02/07/a-critique-of-ally-politics/; McKenzie, M. (2014). *Black Girl Dangerous: On Race, Queerness, Class and Gender.* Oakland, CA: BGD; Utt, J. (Nov. 8, 2013). "So You Call Yourself an Ally: 10 Things All 'Allies' Need to Know." Retrieved from:

http://everydayfeminism.com/2013/11/things-allies-need-to-know/;
Anonymous. *Accomplices Not Allies: Abolishing the Ally Industrial Complex.* Indigenous Action Media. Retrieved from: http://www.indigenous action.org/accomplices-not-allies-abolishing-the-ally-industrial-complex/

[11] McKenzie, M. (2014). "8 Ways Not to Be an Ally" and "No More Allies" in *Black Girl Dangerous: On Race, Queerness, Class and Gender.* Oakland, CA: BGD p. 26-30, 138-141

[12] O'Connor, A. (2001). *Poverty Knowledge: Social Science, Social Policy, and the Poor in Twentieth-Century U.S. History.* Princeton, NJ: Princeton University Press.

[13] For example, for an analysis of War on Poverty era academic and political feuds about poverty: Raz, M. (2013). *What's Wrong with the Poor? Psychiatry, Race, and the War on Poverty.* Chapel Hill: University of North Carolina Press.

[14] Beegle, D.M. (2010). *Action Approach Guidebook: Companion to the DVD: Be the Difference: An Action Approach to Educating Students in Poverty.* Tigard, OR: Communication Across Barriers. p. 36

[15] Putnam, R. (2015) *Our Kids: The American Dream in Crisis.* New York: Simon & Schuster.

[16] Ibid. p. 37

[17] Dinsmore, J. (2007). *My Name is Child of God, not "Those People": A First-Person Look at Poverty.* Minneapolis: Augsburg Fortress.

[18] Melnick, L. (2013). "Eligibility for Cash Assistance Programs." St. Paul, MN: Southern Minnesota Regional Legal Services. Retrieved from: http://www.mfsrc.org/Conferences_files/2013_handouts/MAXIS_HANDOUT.pdf

[19] Star Tribune Editorial Board. (June 12, 2017) "No Raise for Minnesota's Poorest Families – Again." Minneapolis, MN: Star Tribune. Retrieved from: http://www.startribune.com/no-raise-for-minnesota-s-poorest-families-again/428044113/

[20] McKnight, J. (1995). *The Careless Society: Community and its Counterfeits.* New York: Basic.

[21] Badger, E. (Jan. 8, 2014). "It's Time to Stop Blaming Poverty on the Decline in Marriage." Washington, D.C.: CityLab. Retrieved from: https://www.city lab.com/life/2014/01/its-time-stop-blaming-poverty-decline-marriage/8046/

[22] Edin, K. & M. Kefalas. (2005). *Promises I Can Keep: Why Poor Women Put Motherhood Before Marriage.* Berkeley, CA: University of California Press.

[23] For instance: O'Connor, A. (2001). *Poverty Knowledge: Social Science, Social Policy, and the Poor in Twentieth-Century U.S. History.* Princeton, NJ: Princeton University Press. p. 14; Putnam, R. (2015) *Our Kids: The American Dream in Crisis.* New York: Simon & Schuster; Wilkinson, R. & K. Pickett. (2009). *The Spirit Level: Why Greater Equality Makes Societies Stronger.* New York: Bloomsbury.

[24] Gans, H. (1995). *The War Against the Poor: The Underclass and Antipoverty Policy.* New York: BasicBooks. p. 24-26

[25] The culture of poverty is not my favorite theory either. While I do believe there can be cultural differences between classes in tastes and lifestyles, I think people from different class backgrounds tend to have a lot more in common than divergent when it comes to fundamental values and goals. And I do believe our class backgrounds can teach us certain patterns of interacting with the world, but these patterns should be seen as largely value neutral, and can be unlearned as easily as they were learned if they turn out to be counterproductive. In the next chapter I will go into more detail on Dr. Donna Beegle's theory of the lessons poverty teaches, which I find far more compelling than the culture of poverty.

[26] O'Connor, A. (2001). *Poverty Knowledge: Social Science, Social Policy, and the Poor in Twentieth-Century U.S. History.* Princeton, NJ: Princeton University Press; also Gans, H. (1995). *The War Against the Poor: The Underclass and Antipoverty Policy.* New York: BasicBooks. p. 24-26

[27] O'Connor, A. (2001). *Poverty Knowledge: Social Science, Social Policy, and the Poor in Twentieth-Century U.S. History.* Princeton, NJ: Princeton University Press. p. 14

[28] Felitti, V. J., R.F. Anda, D. Nordenberg, D.F. Williamson, A.M. Spitz, V. Edwards, . . . J.S. Marks. (1998). Relationship of childhood abuse and household dysfunction to many of the leading causes of death in adults: The adverse childhood experiences (ACE) study. *American Journal of Preventive Medicine, 14*(4), 245. Retrieved from http://www.ncbi.nlm.nih.gov/pubmed/9635069. See also: Nakazawa, D. J. (2015). *Childhood Disrupted: How Your Biography Becomes Your Biology , and How You Can Heal.* New York, NY: Atria.

[29] Nakazawa, D. J. (2015). *Childhood Disrupted: How Your Biography Becomes Your Biology, and How You Can Heal.* New York, NY: Atria. p. 49 - 59

[30] Ibid

[31] Dinsmore, J. (2007). *My Name is Child of God, not "Those People": A First-Person Look at Poverty.* Minneapolis: Augsburg Fortress.

[32] Leondar-Wright, B. (2005). *Class Matters: Cross Class Alliance Building for Middle Class Activists.* Gabriola Island, BC: New Society. p. 141-144

[33] Morgan, E. (Aug. 13, 2014). "21 Reasons Why It Is Not My Responsibility As a Marginalized Individual to Educate You About My Experience: And Why It Is a Dangerous Notion to Think that I Am." Retrieved from: https://medium.com/@schmutzie/why-it-is-not-my-responsibility-as-a-marginalized-individual-to-educate-you-about-my-experience-915b4ec08efd#.4wgx4i608

[34] Utt, J. (Dec. 7, 2012). "How to Talk About Privilege to Someone Who Doesn't Know What That Is." Retrieved from: http://everydayfeminism.com/2012/12/how-to-talk-to-someone-about-privilege/. See also: Ramsey, F. (November 22, 2014). "5 Tips for Being an Ally." (Video). Retrieved from: https://youtu.be/_dg86g-QlM0

[35] Edwards-Levy, A. (June 2, 2015) "Most Americans Think They're Still Middle Class, But Worry They Might Not Be For Long." New York, NY: HuffPost. Retrieved from: http://www.huffingtonpost.com/2015/06/02/middle-class-poll_n_7487868.html

[36] "Houses near a high-scoring public school cost more than $200,000 more than comparable houses near low-scoring schools." Putnam, R. (2015) *Our Kids: The American Dream in Crisis.* New York: Simon & Schuster. p. 164

[37] Putnam, R. (2015) *Our Kids: The American Dream in Crisis.* New York: Simon & Schuster. p. 218-221

[38] Kehlenberg, R. (2005) The Return of "Separate but Equal." In: Lardner, J and D. Smith (Eds.) *Inequality Matters: The Growing Economic Divide in America and Its Poisonous Consequences.* New York: New Press. p. 54-64.

[39] See Step Six for more information on oral versus print communication styles and how they correlate with class.

[40] Freire, P. (1970/2009). *Pedagogy of the Oppressed,* 30th anniversary edition. New York: Continuum. p. 35

[41] Freire, P. (1970/2009). *Pedagogy of the Oppressed,* 30th anniversary edition. New York: Continuum. p. 44

[42] Ibid p. 44

[43] Ibid p. 60

[44] Brown, B. (2010). *The Gifts of Imperfection: Let Go of Who You Think You're Supposed to Be and Embrace Who You Are.* Center City, MN: Hazelden.

[45] Bishop, A. (2002). *Becoming an Ally: Breaking the Cycle of Oppression in People.* (2nd Ed) London, UK: Zed.

[46] Ibid p. 114-115.

[47] Freire, P. (1970/2009). *Pedagogy of the Oppressed,* 30th anniversary edition. New York: Continuum. p. 49

[48] Leondar-Wright, B. (2005). *Class Matters: Cross Class Alliance Building for Middle Class Activists.* Gabriola Island, BC: New Society. p. 141-144

[49] M. (Feb. 7, 2015). "A Critique of Ally Politics." Retrieved from: https://radicalwashtenaw.org/2015/02/07/a-critique-of-ally-politics/

[50] Freire, P. (1970/2009). *Pedagogy of the Oppressed,* 30th anniversary edition. New York: Continuum. p. 56

[51] McKenzie, M. (2014). "4 Ways to Push Back Against Your Privilege" in *Black Girl Dangerous: On Race, Queerness, Class and Gender.* Oakland, CA: BGD p. 112-116.

[52] Freire, P. (1970/2009). *Pedagogy of the Oppressed,* 30th anniversary edition. New York: Continuum. p. 126

[53] Katz, M.B. (2013). *The Undeserving Poor: America's Enduring Confrontation with Poverty* (2nd Ed.) Oxford, UK: Oxford.

[54] Beegle, D.M. (2007). *See Poverty... Be the Difference! Discover the Missing Pieces for Helping People Move Out of Poverty.* Tigard, OR: Communication Across Barriers. P. 45-46

[55] Ibid

[56] hooks, b. (2000). *Where We Stand: Class Matters.* New York: Routledge. p. 122

[57] Ibid p. 53. See also Beegle, D.M. (2007). *Be The Difference: An Action Approach to Educating Students in Poverty* (DVD).

[58] Beegle, D.M. (2007). *See Poverty... Be the Difference! Discover the Missing Pieces for Helping People Move Out of Poverty.* Tigard, OR: Communication Across Barriers. p. 64

[59] For example, see Class Action. "Hall of Shame: Most Classist Comments." Jamaica Plain, MA: Class Action. Retrieved Sept. 4, 2017 from: http://www.classism.org/programs/classist-comment/hall-of-shame-most-classist-comments/

[60] Dinsmore, J. (2007). *My Name is Child of God, not "Those People": A First-Person Look at Poverty.* Minneapolis: Augsburg Fortress. p. 70

[61] Ibid p. 71

[62] Leondar-Wright, B. (2005). *Class Matters: Cross Class Alliance Building for Middle Class Activists.* Gabriola Island, BC: New Society. p. 116-123

[63] Austin, A. (June 2010) "Uneven Pain: Unemployment By Metropolitan Area and Race." *Issue Brief #278.* Washington, DC: Economic Policy Institute.

[64] Brave Heart, M. Y. H. & L.M. DeBruyn. (1998). The American Indian holocaust: Healing historical unresolved grief. *American Indian and Alaska Native Mental Health Research.* 8(2). p. 71

[65] Ibid. See also Duran, E., B. Duran, M.Y.H. Brave Heart, & S. Y. Horse-Davis, (1998). Healing the American Indian soul wound. *International handbook of multigenerational legacies of trauma* (p. 341-354), New York, NY: Plenum.

[66] Danieli, Y., Ed. (1998) *International handbook of multigenerational legacies of trauma.* New York, NY: Plenum.

[67] Brave Heart, M. Y. H. & L.M. DeBruyn. (1998). The American Indian holocaust: Healing historical unresolved grief. *American Indian and Alaska Native Mental Health Research. 8*(2). p. 71

[68] Ibid p. 57-58

[69] See also Duran, E., B. Duran, M.Y.H. Brave Heart, & S. Y. Horse-Davis, (1998). Healing the American Indian soul wound. *International handbook of multigenerational legacies of trauma* (p. 341-354), New York, NY: Plenum. p. 344

[70] Brave Heart, M. Y. H. & L.M. DeBruyn. (1998). The American Indian holocaust: Healing historical unresolved grief. *American Indian and Alaska Native Mental Health Research. 8*(2) p. 63

[71] Ibid p. 70 - 71

[72] Ibid p. 66

[73] Ibid p. 64 - 65

[74] Frankl, V. (1946/2006) *Man's Search for Meaning.* Boston, MA: Beacon.

[75] Kirmayer, L. J., J.P. Gone, & J. Moses. (2014). Rethinking historical trauma. *Transcultural Psychiatry, 51*(3) p. 307-310

[76] Brave Heart, M. Y. H. & L.M. DeBruyn. (1998). The American Indian holocaust: Healing historical unresolved grief. *American Indian and Alaska Native Mental Health Research. 8*(2) p. 66 – 70

[77] Denham, A. (2008). Rethinking Historical Trauma: Narratives of Resilience. *Transcultural Psychiatry, 45*(3). p. 391-414.

[78] Brave Heart, M. Y. H. & L.M. DeBruyn. (1998). The American Indian holocaust: Healing historical unresolved grief. *American Indian and Alaska Native Mental Health Research. 8*(2) p. 71

[79] 47% of those in poverty in 2004 were white, which is a greater proportion than any other racial group. Beegle, D.M. (2007). *See Poverty... Be the Difference! Discover the Missing Pieces for Helping People Move Out of Poverty.* Tigard, OR: Communication Across Barriers. p. 24-25

[80] O'Connor, A. (2001) *Poverty Knowledge: Social Science, Social Policy, and the Poor in Twentieth-Century U.S. History.* Princeton, NJ: Princeton University Press.

[81] Minnesota Department of Human Services (2010). "Welfare in Minnesota: Facts and Figures." Retrieved from: http://kstp.com/kstpImages/flash/images/MN%20Welfare%20Facts.pdf

[82] Utt, J. (Dec. 7, 2012). "How to Talk About Privilege to Someone Who Doesn't Know What That Is." Retrieved from: http://everydayfeminism.com/2012/12/how-to-talk-to-someone-about-privilege/; See also hooks, b. (2000). "White Poverty: The Politics of Invisibility." In *Where We Stand: Class Matters*. New York: Routledge.

[83] Bishop, A. (2002). *Becoming an Ally: Breaking the Cycle of Oppression in People.* (2nd Ed) London, UK: Zed.

[84] Ibid p. 82.

[85] Danieli, Y., Ed. (1998) *International handbook of multigenerational legacies of trauma.* New York, NY: Plenum.

[86] Bishop, A. (2002). *Becoming an Ally: Breaking the Cycle of Oppression in People.* (2nd Ed) London, UK: Zed.

[87] Cross, W.E. (1998). Black Psychological Functioning and the Legacy of Slavery: Myths and Realities. in *International handbook of multigenerational legacies of trauma* (p. 387-400) New York, NY: Plenum. p. 390

[88] Leondar-Wright, B. (2005). *Class Matters: Cross-Class Alliance Building for Middle Class Activists.* Gabriola Island, BC: New Society. p. 12

[89] O'Connor, A. (2001) *Poverty Knowledge: Social Science, Social Policy, and the Poor in Twentieth-Century U.S. History.* Princeton, NJ: Princeton University Press.

[90] Kenrick, D.T., S.L Neuberg, & R.B Cialdini. (2002). *Social Psychology: Unraveling the Mystery.* Boston, MA: Allyn & Bacon. p. 92 & 498.

[91] Ibid p. 81-82.

[92] Additionally, collectivist cultures are less likely to demonstrate the "fundamental" attribution error either. Ibid p. 83.

[93] Beegle, D.M. (2007). *Be The Difference: An Action Approach to Educating Students in Poverty* (DVD)

[94] Putnam, R. (2015) *Our Kids: The American Dream in Crisis.* New York: Simon & Schuster. p. 163-190

[95] Beegle, D.M. (2007). *Be The Difference: An Action Approach to Educating Students in Poverty* (DVD).

[96] Rios, C. (March 30, 2016). "7 Reasons We Have to Stop Treating "Poor" Like a Bad Word." Retrieved from: http://everydayfeminism.com/2016/03/treating-poor-like-bad-word/

[97] Brown, B. (2015). *Rising Strong: How the Ability to Reset Transforms the Way We Live, Love, Parent and Lead.* New York, NY: Random House. p. 119 See also note 44.

[98] Kenrick, D.T., S.L Neuberg, & R.B Cialdini. (2002). *Social Psychology: Unraveling the Mystery.* Boston, MA: Allyn & Bacon. p. 90-92.

[99] Wilkinson, R. & K. Pickett. (2009). *The Spirit Level: Why Greater Equality Makes Societies Stronger.* New York, NY: Bloomsbury.

[100] Beegle, D.M. (2010). *Action Approach Guidebook: Companion to the DVD: Be the Difference: An Action Approach to Educating Students in Poverty.* Tigard, OR: Communication Across Barriers. p. 36

[101] Kenrick, D.T., S.L Neuberg, & R.B Cialdini. (2002). *Social Psychology: Unraveling the Mystery.* Boston, MA: Allyn & Bacon. p. 92 & 498.

[102] Beegle, D.M. (2010). *Action Approach Guidebook: Companion to the DVD: Be the Difference: An Action Approach to Educating Students in Poverty.* Tigard, OR: Communication Across Barriers.

[103] "Once a situation of violence and oppression has been established, it engenders an entire way of life and behavior for those caught up in it—oppressors and oppressed alike. Both are submerged in this situation, and both bear the marks of oppression." Freire, P. (1970/2009). *Pedagogy of the Oppressed,* 30th anniversary edition. New York, NY: Continuum. p. 58

[104] For instance, regarding the word "queer:" Higgins, M. (2016). "Is the Word 'Queer' Offensive? Here's a Look at its History in the LGBTQA+ Community." Retrieved from: https://www.bustle.com/articles/139727-is-the-word-queer-offensive-heres-a-look-at-its-history-in-the-lgbtqa-community

[105] Baptist, W. & J. Rehmann. (2011) *Pedagogy of the Poor: Building the Movement to End Poverty.* New York, NY: Teachers College Press.

[106] Freire, P. (1970/2009). *Pedagogy of the Oppressed,* 30th anniversary edition. New York: Continuum. p. 45

[107] Freire continues: "For them [the oppressors], *having more* is an inalienable right, a right they acquired through their own "effort," with their "courage to take risks." If others do not have more, it is because they are incompetent and lazy, and worst of all is their unjustifiable ingratitude towards the "generous gestures" of the dominant class. Precisely because they are "ungrateful" and "envious," the oppressed are regarded as potential enemies who must be watched." Ibid p. 59

[108] Ibid p. 58

[109] Wilkinson, R. and K. Pickett. (2009). *The Spirit Level: Why Greater Equality Makes Societies Stronger.* New York: Bloomsbury. p. 8.

[110] Freire, P. (1970/2009). *Pedagogy of the Oppressed,* 30th anniversary edition. New York: Continuum. p. 46

[111] Research has shown that societies with a high level of inequality tend to be more materialistic among all economic strata. Frank, R. (2005). How the Middle Class Is Injured by Gains at the Top. In: Lardner, J and D. Smith (Eds.) *Inequality Matters: The Growing Economic Divide in America and Its Poisonous Consequences.* New York: New Press. p. 138 – 149.

[112] hooks, b. (2000). *Where We Stand: Class Matters.* New York: Routledge. p. 46

[113] For example: Mistler, S. (Nov. 23, 2015) "Maine DHHS renews push for ban on buying soda and candy with food stamps." Portland, ME: Portland Press Herald. Retrieved from: http://www.pressherald.com/2015/11/23/maine-renews-push-to-prohibit-food-stamp-recipients-from-purchasing-soda-and-candy/

[114] Beegle, D.M. (2007). *Be The Difference: An Action Approach to Educating Students in Poverty* (DVD)

[115] Freire, P. (1970/2009). *Pedagogy of the Oppressed,* 30th anniversary edition. New York: Continuum. p. 152

[116] Ibid p. 49

[117] McKenzie, M. (2014). *Black Girl Dangerous: On Race, Queerness, Class and Gender.* Oakland, CA: BGD. p. 161

[118] Ibid. p. 156.

[119] Freire, P. (1970/2009). *Pedagogy of the Oppressed,* 30th anniversary edition. New York: Continuum. p. 60

[120] Utt, J. (Feb. 8, 2016). "5 Ways to Avoid Common Ally Pitfalls by Learning From Your Mistakes" Retrieved from: https://everydayfeminism.com/2016/02/learn-about-allyship-mistakes/

[121] Ostrove, J. & G. Oliva. (2010). Identifying Allies: Explorations of Deaf-Hearing Relationships. In S. Burch & A Kafer (Eds) *Deaf and Disability Studies: Interdisciplinary Perspectives.* Washington, DC: Gallaudet University.

[122] Beegle, D.M. (2007). *Be The Difference: An Action Approach to Educating Students in Poverty* (DVD)

[123] Ibid

[124] Beegle, D.M. (2007). *See Poverty... Be the Difference! Discover the Missing Pieces for Helping People Move Out of Poverty.* Tigard, OR: Communication Across Barriers. p. 150

[125] Ibid, p. 150

[126] Ibid p. 53. See also previous discussion in Step Two.

[127] Dinsmore, J. (2007). *My Name is Child of God, not "Those People": A First-Person Look at Poverty.* Minneapolis: Augsburg Fortress. p. 165-166

[128] Perry, S. (2014). Wage Fight Poses Dilemma for Nonprofits Squeezed by State Funding. *Chronicle Of Philanthropy, 26*(13), 2.

[129] For example, the federal government has estimated that the average 200-employee Wal-Mart store costs the government $420,750 annually for assistance given to its employees, roughly $2,103 per employee. From: Ehrenreich, B. (2005). Earth to Wal-Mars. In: Lardner, J and D. Smith (Eds.)

Inequality Matters: The Growing Economic Divide in America and Its Poisonous Consequences. New York, NY: New Press. p. 50.

[130] Beegle, D.M. (2007). *See Poverty… Be the Difference! Discover the Missing Pieces for Helping People Move Out of Poverty.* Tigard, OR: Communication Across Barriers. p. 150

[131] Putnam, R. (2015) *Our Kids: The American Dream in Crisis.* New York: Simon & Schuster.

[132] Beegle, D.M. (2010). *Action Approach Guidebook: Companion to the DVD: Be the Difference: An Action Approach to Educating Students in Poverty.* Tigard, OR: Communication Across Barriers. p. 36

[133] Ostrove, J. M. & S.M. Long. (2007). Social Class and Belonging: Implications for College Adjustment. *The Review of Higher Education. 30*(4), 363-389.

[134] Stout, L. (1996). *Bridging the Class Divide and other Lessons for Grassroots Organizing.* Boston: Beacon. p. 23; Beegle, D.M. (2007). *See Poverty… Be the Difference! Discover the Missing Pieces for Helping People Move Out of Poverty.* Tigard, OR: Communication Across Barriers. p. 12.

[135] Morgan, E. (Aug. 13, 2014). "21 Reasons Why It Is Not My Responsibility As a Marginalized Individual to Educate You About My Experience: And Why It Is a Dangerous Notion to Think that I Am." Retrieved from: https://medium.com/@schmutzie/why-it-is-not-my-responsibility-as-a-marginalized-individual-to-educate-you-about-my-experience-915b4ec08efd#.4wgx4i608

[136] This is just one example of the double standards of moral behavior, where the poor are often used as scapegoats to justify moral outrage among middle or owning-class people who simultaneously don't hold themselves to the same moral standards. See: Gans, H. (1995). *The War Against the Poor: The Underclass and Antipoverty Policy.* New York: BasicBooks. p. 84

[137] Freire, P. (1970/2009). *Pedagogy of the Oppressed,* 30th anniversary edition. New York: Continuum. p. 44

[138] Beegle, D.M. (2007). *See Poverty… Be the Difference! Discover the Missing Pieces for Helping People Move Out of Poverty.* Tigard, OR: Communication Across Barriers. p. 53-54

[139] For example, in the mid-twentieth century, "armed with an every-expanding battery of psychological tests and developmental theories, social scientists were now 'diagnosing' behaviors once viewed as cultural adaptations as deeply ingrained personality traits. The lower-class penchant for immediate gratification offers a case in point. Viewed by sympathetic anthropologists as a reasonable response to deprivation—why wait to enjoy

what might not be there tomorrow?—by the 1950s the 'inability to defer gratification' had been transformed into a certifiable personality disorder." O'Connor, A. (2001) *Poverty Knowledge: Social Science, Social Policy, and the Poor in Twentieth-Century U.S. History.* Princeton, NJ: Princeton University Press. p. 109

[140] Leondar-Wright, B. (2005). *Class Matters: Cross Class Alliance Building for Middle Class Activists.* Gabriola Island, BC: New Society. p. 141-144

[141] Dinsmore, J. (2007). *My Name is Child of God, not "Those People": A First-Person Look at Poverty.* Minneapolis: Augsburg Fortress. p. 63-66.

[142] Dinsmore, J. (2007). *My Name is Child of God, not "Those People": A First-Person Look at Poverty.* Minneapolis: Augsburg Fortress. p. 20-21.

[143] Belenky, M.F., B. McV. Clincy, N. R. Goldberger, & J. M. Tarule (1986/1997). *Women's Ways of Knowing: The Development of Self, Voice, and Mind,* 10th anniversary edition. New York, NY: Basic Books. See also Belenky, M. F., L. A. Bond, & J. S. Weinstock (1997). *A Tradition that Has No Name: Nurturing the Development of People, Families, and Communities.* New York, NY: Basic Books. p. 58-62

[144] Freire, P. (1970/2009). *Pedagogy of the Oppressed,* 30th anniversary edition. New York, NY: Continuum. p. 126.

[145] Belenky, M. F., L. A. Bond, & J. S. Weinstock (1997). *A Tradition that Has No Name: Nurturing the Development of People, Families, and Communities.* New York, NY: Basic Books. p. 258 – 292.

[146] Ramsey, F. (November 22, 2014). "5 Tips for Being an Ally." (Video). Retrieved from: https://youtu.be/ dg86g-QIM0

[147] McKenzie, M. (2014). "4 Ways to Push Back Against Your Privilege" in *Black Girl Dangerous: On Race, Queerness, Class and Gender.* Oakland, CA: BGD p. 114-115.

[148] Belenky, M. F., L. A. Bond, & J. S. Weinstock (1997). *A Tradition that Has No Name: Nurturing the Development of People, Families, and Communities.* New York, NY: Basic Books. P. 273.

[149] Ibid

[150] Ibid p. 13

[151] Ibid p. 266

[152] Ibid p. 269

[153] Ibid p. 274-275

[154] Ibid p. 13

[155] "Most of the homeplace women we studied rejected leadership organized around patriarchal notions. Most were very critical of using the doctor-patient relationship as a model for working with people. They also

avoided the language of the social services and the helping professions. To them people were neither "patients" to be "treated" or "cured" nor "clients" to be "serviced" or "helped." Instead, the homeplace women see themselves more like mothers who create nurturing families that support the growth and development of people and communities." Ibid p. 261

[156] Ibid p. 292

[157] Ibid p. 287

[158] Ibid p. 283

[159] Ibid p. 273

[160] Freire, P. (1970/2009). *Pedagogy of the Oppressed,* 30th anniversary edition. New York, NY: Continuum. p. 126.

[161] Le, V. (2013). "Being a Nonprofit With Balls, Part 2." Retrieved from: http://nonprofitwithballs.com/2013/01/being-a-nonprofit-with-balls-part-2/

[162] Ibid

[163] Horton, M. & P. Freire. (Eds.) B. Bell, J. Gaventa, & J. Peters. (1990). *We Make the Road by Walking: Conversations on Education and Social Change.* Philadelphia, PA: Temple University. p. 135

[164] Belenky, M. F., L. A. Bond, & J. S. Weinstock (1997). *A Tradition that Has No Name: Nurturing the Development of People, Families, and Communities.* New York, NY: Basic Books. p. 10, 229-257.

[165] Utt, J. (Nov. 8, 2013). "So You Call Yourself an Ally: 10 Things All 'Allies' Need to Know." Retrieved from: http://everydayfeminism.com/2013/11/things-allies-need-to-know/

[166] Utt, J. (Nov. 8, 2013). "So You Call Yourself an Ally: 10 Things All 'Allies' Need to Know." Retrieved from: http://everydayfeminism.com/2013/11/things-allies-need-to-know/

[167] Duran, E., B. Duran, M.Y.H. Brave Heart, & S. Y. Horse-Davis, (1998). Healing the American Indian soul wound. *International handbook of multigenerational legacies of trauma* (p. 341-354), New York, NY: Plenum.

[168] Dinsmore, J. (2007). *My Name is Child of God, not "Those People": A First-Person Look at Poverty.* Minneapolis: Augsburg Fortress. p. 19

[169] Ibid p. 146

[170] Edkins, J. & M. Zehfuss, (Eds.) (2014) *Global Politics: A New Introduction.* (2nd Ed.) London, UK: Routledge. p. 602-603.

[171] O'Connor, A. (2001) *Poverty Knowledge: Social Science, Social Policy, and the Poor in Twentieth-Century U.S. History.* Princeton, NJ: Princeton. p. 196-210

[172] Gans, H. (1995). *The War Against the Poor: The Underclass and Antipoverty Policy.* New York, NY: BasicBooks. p. 24-26

[173] Leondar-Wright, B. (2005). *Class Matters: Cross-Class Alliance Building for Middle Class Activists.* Gabriola Island, BC: New Society. p. 89

[174] The Mall of America has since relaxed its grooming standards. The current requirements can be viewed here: www.nickelodeonuniverse.com/employment

[175] Freire, P. (1970/2009). *Pedagogy of the Oppressed,* 30th anniversary edition. New York, NY: Continuum. p. 153

[176] Ibid p. 153

[177] Isenberg, N. (2016). *White Trash: The 400-Year Untold History of Class in America.* New York, NY: Viking. p. 307-308

[178] Demby, G. (April 8, 2013). "How Code-Switching Explains the World." Washington, D.C.: NPR. Retrieved from: http://www.npr.org/blogs/codeswitch/2013/04/02/176064688/how-code-switching-explains-the-world

[179] Beegle, D.M. (2007). *See Poverty... Be the Difference! Discover the Missing Pieces for Helping People Move Out of Poverty.* Tigard, OR: Communication Across Barriers. p. 97

[180] Ibid p. 97

[181] Beegle, D.M. (2007). *Be The Difference: An Action Approach to Educating Students in Poverty* (DVD)

[182] Beegle, D.M. (2007). *See Poverty... Be the Difference! Discover the Missing Pieces for Helping People Move Out of Poverty.* Tigard, OR: Communication Across Barriers. p. 98-99

[183] Ibid p. 98-99

[184] Ibid p. 98

[185] Ibid p. 98

[186] Personal correspondence with Julia Dinsmore (Sept. 2017).

[187] Beegle, D.M. (2007). *See Poverty... Be the Difference! Discover the Missing Pieces for Helping People Move Out of Poverty.* Tigard, OR: Communication Across Barriers. p. 110

[188] Ibid p. 108-122

[189] Duran, E., B. Duran, M.Y.H. Brave Heart, & S. Y. Horse-Davis, (1998). Healing the American Indian soul wound. *International handbook of multigenerational legacies of trauma* (p. 341-354), New York, NY: Plenum. p. 345

[190] Anner, J. As quoted in B. Leondar-Wright. (2005). *Class Matters: Cross Class Alliance Building for Middle Class Activists.* Gabriola Island, BC: New Society. p. 106

191 Because A Minnesota Without Poverty was at that time a faith-based ecumenical organization, we used a version of Strengths Finder customized for churches. Winseman, A.L; D. O. Clifton & C. Liesveld (2004). *Living Your Strengths: Discover Your God-Given Talents and Inspire Your Community.* New York, NY: Gallup. A more general form of the Strengths Finder assessment and classification system can be found here: Rath, T. (2007). *Strengths Finder 2.0.* New York, NY: Gallup.

192 Winseman, A.L; D. O. Clifton & C. Liesveld (2004). *Living Your Strengths: Discover Your God-Given Talents and Inspire Your Community.* New York, NY: Gallup.

193 Horton, M. & P. Freire. (Eds.) B. Bell, J. Gaventa, & J. Peters. (1990). *We Make the Road by Walking: Conversations on Education and Social Change.* Philadelphia: Temple University Press.

194 Ibid p. 115-128

195 Ibid p. 116

196 Stout, L. (2011). *Collective Visioning: How Groups Can Work Together for a Just and Sustainable Future.* San Francisco: Berrett-Koehler. p. 115.

197 Ibid, p. 108-114

198 Freire, P. (1970/2009). *Pedagogy of the Oppressed,* 30th anniversary edition. New York: Continuum. p 125

199 Ibid p. 65, p. 100-101, p. 125

200 Ibid p. 35

201 Ibid p. 66

202 Ibid p. 126

203 Ibid p. 126

204 Belenky, M. F., L. A. Bond, and J. S. Weinstock (1997). *A Tradition that Has No Name: Nurturing the Development of People, Families, and Communities.* New York: Basic Books. p. 266 – 275. And Freire, P. (1970/2009). *Pedagogy of the Oppressed,* 30th anniversary edition. New York: Continuum.

205 Freire, P. (1970/2009). *Pedagogy of the Oppressed,* 30th anniversary edition. New York, NY: Continuum; See also Brookfield, S.D. (2004). *The Power of Critical Theory: Liberating Adult Learning and Teaching.* San Francisco, CA: Jossey-Bass

206 Freire, P. (1970/2009). *Pedagogy of the Oppressed,* 30th anniversary edition. New York, NY: Continuum. p 66

207 For a defense of Freire's writing style, see the introduction to the 30th Anniversary edition. Freire, P. (1970/2009). *Pedagogy of the Oppressed,* 30th anniversary edition. New York, NY: Continuum. p 23

208 Ibid p. 114-117

[209] Beegle, D.M. (2007). *See Poverty... Be the Difference! Discover the Missing Pieces for Helping People Move Out of Poverty.* Tigard, OR: Communication Across Barriers. p. 87-91

[210] Beegle, D.M. (2007). *Be The Difference: An Action Approach to Educating Students in Poverty* (DVD)

[211] Brown, V. P. (2004). *The Education of Jane Addams.* Philadelphia, PA: U of Pennsylvania. p. 4

[212] Ibid p. 263 - 270

[213] Segal, N. "Jane Addams of Hull House." New York NY: Junior Scholastic. Retrieved from: http://www.scholastic.com/browse/article.jsp?id=4948 and Davis, A. F. (1973/2000) *American Heroine: The Life and Legend of Jane Addams.* Chicago, IL: Ivan R. Dee.

[214] Davis, A. F. (1973/2000) *American Heroine: The Life and Legend of Jane Addams.* Chicago: Ivan R. Dee. p. 65

[215] Brown, V. P. (2004). *The Education of Jane Addams.* Philadelphia, PA: U of Pennsylvania.

[216] Ellen Gates Starr, Jane Addams' partner in starting the Hull House, wrote that "Jane's idea, which she... on no account will give up, is that [the settlement house] is more for the benefit of the people who do it than for the other class." Knight, L. W. (2005). *Citizen: Jane Addams and the Struggle for Democracy.* Chicago, IL: U of Chicago. p. 182

[217] Ibid p. 66-67

[218] Shah, A. (Jan. 7, 2013) "Poverty Facts and Stats." Retrieved from: http://www.globalissues.org/article/26/poverty-facts-and-stats

[219] Gans, H. (1995). *The War Against the Poor: The Underclass and Antipoverty Policy.* New York, NY: BasicBooks. p.91-102

[220] Ibid p. 97

[221] Ibid p. 94. See also discussions of the poverty industry in Step One and Step Four.

[222] Ibid p. 91

[223] Freire, P. (1970/2009). *Pedagogy of the Oppressed,* 30th anniversary edition. New York: Continuum. p. 56

[224] For a good resource on developing this kind of positive vision individually or with a group, see Stout, L. (2011). *Collective Visioning: How Groups Can Work Together for a Just and Sustainable Future.* San Francisco, CA: Berrett-Koehler.

[225] Wilkinson, R. & K. Pickett. (2009). *The Spirit Level: Why Greater Equality Makes Societies Stronger.* New York: Bloomsbury p. 25

[226] Ibid

[227] Ibid p. 5-10

228 Wilkinson, R. & K. Pickett. (2009). *The Spirit Level: Why Greater Equality Makes Societies Stronger.* New York: Bloomsbury p. 20-23

229 Ibid p. 181

230 Ibid See especially p. 31-45

231 Ibid p. 166-167.

232 Gans, H. (1995). *The War Against the Poor: The Underclass and Antipoverty Policy.* New York, NY: BasicBooks. p.91-102

233 This activity does rely on some questionable statistics, and I don't recall the particulars of the version used in the exercise in which I participated, but the sentiment is still valuable. See a discussion of accuracy: Mikkelson, D. (April 7, 2015) "Earth Population as a Village of 100 People." Retrieved from: http://www.snopes.com/science/stats/populate.asp

234 Ehrenreich, B. (2001). *Nickel and Dimed: On (Not) Getting By in America.* New York, NY: Henry Holt.

235 Bousehey H & C. Weller. (2005). What the Numbers Tell Us. In: Lardner, J and D. Smith (Eds.) *Inequality Matters: The Growing Economic Divide in America and Its Poisonous Consequences.* New York, NY: New Press. p. 36.

236 Greider, W. (2005). Building a Moral Economy. In: Lardner, J and D. Smith (Eds.) *Inequality Matters: The Growing Economic Divide in America and Its Poisonous Consequences.* New York: New Press. p. 251.

237 "Novice." *Dictionary.com Unabridged.* Random House, Inc. Retrieved on Dec. 20, 2016 from: http://www.dictionary.com/browse/novice

238 Freire, P. (1970/2009). *Pedagogy of the Oppressed,* 30th anniversary edition. New York, NY: Continuum. p 129

239 For example: M. (Feb. 7, 2015). "A Critique of Ally Politics." Retrieved from: https://radicalwashtenaw.org/2015/02/07/a-critique-of-ally-politics/; McKenzie, M. (2014). *Black Girl Dangerous: On Race, Queerness, Class and Gender.* Oakland, CA: BGD; Utt, J. (Nov. 8, 2013). "So You Call Yourself an Ally: 10 Things All 'Allies' Need to Know." Retrieved from: http://everydayfeminism.com/2013/11/things-allies-need-to-know/; Anonymous. *Accomplices Not Allies: Abolishing the Ally Industrial Complex.* Indigenous Action Media. http://www.indigenousaction.org/accomplices-not-allies-abolishing-the-ally-industrial-complex/

240 McKenzie, M. (2014). "No More Allies" in *Black Girl Dangerous: On Race, Queerness, Class and Gender.* Oakland, CA: BGD p. 140.

241 Utt, J. (Nov. 8, 2013). "So You Call Yourself an Ally: 10 Things All 'Allies' Need to Know." Retrieved from: http://everydayfeminism.com/2013/11/things-allies-need-to-know/

242 M. (Feb. 7, 2015). "A Critique of Ally Politics." Retrieved from: https://radicalwashtenaw.org/2015/02/07/a-critique-of-ally-politics/

243 M. (Feb. 7, 2015). "A Critique of Ally Politics." Retrieved from: https://radicalwashtenaw.org/2015/02/07/a-critique-of-ally-politics/

244 Leondar-Wright, B. (2005). *Class Matters: Cross Class Alliance Building for Middle Class Activists.* Gabriola Island, BC: New Society. p. 141-144

245 M. (Feb. 7, 2015). "A Critique of Ally Politics." Retrieved from: https://radicalwashtenaw.org/2015/02/07/a-critique-of-ally-politics/

246 Anonymous. *Accomplices Not Allies: Abolishing the Ally Industrial Complex.* Indigenous Action Media. http://www.indigenous action.org/accomplices-not-allies-abolishing-the-ally-industrial-complex/

247 M. (Feb. 7, 2015). "A Critique of Ally Politics." Retrieved from: https://radicalwashtenaw.org/2015/02/07/a-critique-of-ally-politics/

248 Utt, J. (Nov. 8, 2013). "So You Call Yourself an Ally: 10 Things All 'Allies' Need to Know." Retrieved from: http://everydayfeminism.com/2013/11/things-allies-need-to-know/

249 M. (Feb. 7, 2015). "A Critique of Ally Politics." Retrieved from: https://radicalwashtenaw.org/2015/02/07/a-critique-of-ally-politics/

250 Anonymous. *Accomplices Not Allies: Abolishing the Ally Industrial Complex.* Indigenous Action Media. http://www.indigenous action.org/accomplices-not-allies-abolishing-the-ally-industrial-complex/

251 McKenzie, M. (2014). "No More Allies" in *Black Girl Dangerous: On Race, Queerness, Class and Gender.* Oakland, CA: BGD p. 138.

252 Ibid. p. 139.

253 M. (Feb. 7, 2015). "A Critique of Ally Politics." Retrieved from: https://radicalwashtenaw.org/2015/02/07/a-critique-of-ally-politics/

254 Belenky, M. F., L. A. Bond, & J. S. Weinstock (1997). *A Tradition that Has No Name: Nurturing the Development of People, Families, and Communities.* New York, NY: Basic Books.

255 Marcus, Sara. (July 2004). "Why Politics and Purity Don't Mix." Utne Reader, 78-81. Retrieved from: http://proxying.lib.ncsu.edu/index.php?url=http://search.proquest.com/docview/217416627?accountid=12725